THE FOOTBALL ENCYCLOPEDIA

CLIVE GIFFORD

KINGFISHER

KINGFISHER

Published 2018 by Kingfisher
an imprint of Macmillan Children's Books
20 New Wharf Road, London N1 9RR
Associated companies throughout the world
www.panmacmillan.com

Consultant: Anthony Hobbs
Cover design: Matthew Kelly

ISBN 978-0-7534-4223-4

First published in 2006 by Kingfisher
This fully revised and updated edition published
2018 by Kingfisher

9 8 7 6 5 4 3
3TR/1118/WKT/UG/128MA

A CIP catalogue record for this book is available from
the British Library.

Printed in China

Note to readers: The website addresses listed in
this book are correct at the time of publishing. However,
due to the ever-changing nature of the internet, website
addresses and content can change. Websites can contain
links that are unsuitable for children. The publisher cannot
be held responsible for changes in website addresses or
content, or for information obtained through third-party
websites. We strongly advise that internet searches
should be supervised by an adult.

THE
FOOTBALL
ENCYCLOPEDIA

Brazil and England contest their 2002 World Cup quarter-final in Japan's Shizuoka Stadium Ecopa. The 50,600-capacity arena hosts the bigger matches of two Japanese J-League sides, Jubilo Iwata and Shimizu S-Pulse.

CONTENTS

THE BEAUTIFUL GAME

Pelé described football as the 'beautiful game', and the emotion and loyalty football inspires in its fans means that this simple sport has much to live up to. But football delivers with ease – cramming dynamic action, breathtaking skills and heartstopping tension into 90 minutes of play. It is sport as drama, making heroes and villains out of its players, managers and officials. From its recognized beginnings in the 19th century to its global dominance today, football has provided great moments of excitement, celebration and despair; no other game has the same power to unite and divide.

RAPID GROWTH

In little over a century, football has boomed from a casual pursuit carried out by a small group of amateur gentlemen to a highly sophisticated, money-spinning sport that is played and watched by millions of people. As football has grown, dozens of changes have occurred. Some have involved the laws of the game – from the two-handed throw-in, introduced in 1883, to the backpass law for goalkeepers that was adopted 99 years later. Other changes – such as the arrival of promotion and relegation up and down a league – have shaped the competitions of which matches are a part.

Football's adaptability has been one of its strengths. Another great part of its appeal is that people of all ages and skill levels can play the game. At its most basic, football is a simple sport that can be enjoyed without expensive equipment and played almost anywhere – from a sandy beach to an office or hallway with a crumpled ball of paper.

The simplicity of football is a big selling point with new fans. The finer details of rules and tactics may pass them by at first, but the basics of the game and the skills of star players – their pace, ball control, passing, shooting and tackling – can be admired by almost anyone.

▲ Football is a sport that generates intensely strong bonds between supporters and their teams. This fan, facepainted in the national colours of Portugal, awaits an international match against the Netherlands.

▼ Football arouses the emotions of players as well as fans. Here, Bayern Munich's Carsten Jancker (left) and Thomas Helmer are inconsolable after their team was beaten by Manchester United in the last minute of the 1999 Champions League final.

▼ Argentina and Barcelona star Lionel Messi (front) battles for the ball with Manchester United's Michael Carrick during a Champions League game. Outrageously skilful, Messi was voted the world's best player for four years in a row (2009–12) and again in 2015.

▲ Football can be played practically anywhere, in almost any conditions. These South African schoolchildren are enjoying a casual game just days before their country hosted the 2010 World Cup.

THE NUMBERS GAME

In its full version, football is a game in which two teams of 11 people play two halves of 45 minutes. Today, more than 50 million footballers around the world play in official competitions. Many millions more play the game on a regular basis – a survey by world football's governing body, the *Fédération Internationale de Football Association* (FIFA), estimates that figure to be more than 265 million. Top leagues, such as Serie A in Italy, Spain's La Liga and Germany's Bundesliga, attract millions of viewers. In 2017, English Premier League games or highlights were broadcast to more than 190 countries. Each of the 2014 World Cup's 64 matches was watched by an average TV audience of around a million, while the 2014 final attracted almost one billion viewers.

▲ A Brazilian goalkeeper holds a commemorative football celebrating Brazil's successful bid to host the FIFA World Cup for the first time since 1950. Major tournaments generate huge interest and millions are spent on stadiums and facilities for the huge numbers of visiting fans.

THEN AND NOW

Going back in time 140 years, a modern football fan would be surprised to find no referees, corners or pitch markings at a game. Players wore coats and even top hats; they handled the ball in the air and wrestled with each other on the ground. Over time, football has evolved into the game that we know today.

▶ The referee's whistle was first blown at a football match in 1878. British firm Acme Whistles, astonishingly, has sold over 200 million Acme Thunderer whistles, which have been heard at World Cups and in top leagues around the globe.

PITCHING UP

Unlike in most sports, the pitch in football can vary in size. Most are around 100m long and 65–70m wide. Back in the 1860s, a pitch could be as long as 180m. The first markings arrived in 1891, including a centre circle and a line running the width of the pitch, 10.98m in front of the goal line. A penalty could be taken from any point along that line. It was another 11 years before the pitch markings we know today were introduced. Since then, only two additions have been made – the penalty arc at the front of the penalty area (in 1937) and the corner quadrants (in 1938).

▶ Referee Ken Aston came up with the idea of red and yellow cards after a stormy World Cup game in 1966. Here, he sends off Italy's Georgio Ferrini in 1962.

▲ At the 2002 World Cup, held in Japan and South Korea, the grass at the Sapporo Dome was grown away from the stadium and then moved as an entire pitch into the arena on a cushion of air.

GOALS

To score a goal, a team has to propel the whole of the ball over the goal line, between two posts that are set 7.32m apart. On many occasions, controversy has raged over whether the ball crossed the line – from the 1966 World Cup final between England and West Germany to the DFB-Pokal Cup final in 2014 between Borussia Dortmund and Bayern Munich.

Early goals consisted of just two posts. Following arguments over the height of a shot, a white tape was fitted to the posts, 2.44m above the ground. Wooden crossbars began to replace tape in the 1870s. Goal nets came later, invented by an engineer from Liverpool, John Alexander Brodie.

THE MEN (AND WOMEN) IN BLACK

Referees did not feature in early games of football because the sport's founders believed that gentlemen would never intentionally foul or cheat. Instead, each side had an umpire to whom they could appeal. By 1891, games were controlled by a referee in order to cut down on controversial decisions and long stoppages for debate, and the two umpires became linesmen. (Since 1996, linesmen have been known as assistants.) Despite often being described as the 'men in black', referees have played in all sorts of colours. Early referees tried to keep up with play dressed in the popular fashions of the time – trousers, a blazer and even a bow tie.

They were first given a trial in January 1891, when Everton's Fred Geary became the first footballer to put the ball in the back of the net. Incidentally, that game was refereed by Sam Widdowson, who had invented shinpads 17 years earlier.

FACTFILE The Belgian referee at the 1930 World Cup final, Jean Langenus, wore a dinner jacket, golfing plus-four trousers and a red striped tie.

BOOTS AND BALLS

No game is complete without the football, 40 million of which are sold every year. It is the referee's job to check the match ball and spare balls for size (68–70cm), weight (410–450 grams) and correct air pressure. Modern footballs are made from leather or synthetic materials, with a waterproof outer coating. Brazilian club Santos pioneered the use of a white ball (instead of the traditional brown leather ball) for greater visibility during evening games. Early footballs were made from the inflated bladder of a pig or sheep, covered in a leather shell that was secured with a set of laces. Contrary to popular myth, footballs of the past were not heavier than today's, at least when they were dry. Without a waterproof covering, however, early balls soaked up moisture and gained weight.

Football boots were certainly heavier in the past. Originally, players used their heavy work boots, tying them up over the ankle. The boots often had reinforced toecaps, and players sometimes nailed metal or leather studs into the soles. Modern boots are lightweight and flexible, allowing a player to 'feel' the ball on his or her foot. Their soles come in a range of stud, dimple and blade patterns. Each design gives the right level of grip for a particular pitch condition.

FACTFILE

India withdrew from the 1950 World Cup when FIFA refused to allow their footballers to play in bare feet.

▲ Some modern boots have moulded dimples for playing on hard or artificial pitches; others have screw-in studs to give grip on wet or soft pitches.

▲ Alex James, a star for Arsenal in the 1930s, tries out a muscle-enhancing machine. Today's players undergo carefully planned exercise regimes and eat a diet that is scientifically monitored by their clubs.

KITTED OUT

Today's lightweight football kits are the result of years of research and development. During the first ever international fixture, in 1872, the Scotland and England teams wore knickerbockers (long trousers), long shirts and bobble hats or caps. Gradually, football kit developed to give players more freedom of movement, although shorts remained almost knee length until the 1960s. Numbers appeared on shirts regularly for the first time in the 1930s, but player names did not arrive until the late 1980s. In 1924, the English Football Association (FA) began to insist that teams have a second strip (known as an away strip) that could be worn in the event of a colour clash. Today, kit manufacture is a highly profitable business. Teams often have two or even three away strips; they update their kit design every season and sell many thousands of replica shirts to supporters.

▼ Samuel Eto'o wears Cameroon's radical all-in-one kit at the 2004 African Nations Cup. The figure-hugging design gave opponents little material to tug or pull, but broke FIFA's rule that shirts and shorts have to be separate. An earlier Cameroon kit with sleeveless shirts – worn for the 2002 World Cup qualifying games – was also declared illegal.

FOOTBALL'S ORIGINS

An alehouse in Victorian England seems an unlikely place to launch a sport that would become the world's biggest and most popular. Yet that is precisely what occurred in 1863 at the Freemason's Tavern in London, England. There, representatives of 12 clubs met to form the Football Association (FA) and draw up a single set of rules for the game.

HISTORY MYSTERY

No one knows where the first forerunner of football was played. The Ancient Greeks took part in a team ball game known as *episkyros* or *pheninda*, while the Romans played *harpastum*. Paintings dating back more than 2,000 years show men and women enjoying the Ancient Chinese game of *tsu chu*, in which players tried to propel a ball made of stuffed animal skin through bamboo goal posts up to 10m tall. During the Ch'in dynasty (255–206BCE), a form of *tsu chu* was used to help train soldiers.

In medieval Europe, games of mob football were so unruly and violent that the leaders of several countries, including Charles V in France and Oliver Cromwell in England, attempted to ban the sport. In contrast to mob football, the Italian game of *calcio* was first played in the 16th century by aristocrats and religious leaders, including three popes. Each team was made up of 27 players, and goals were scored by kicking or throwing the ball over a certain spot on the edge of the field.

GETTING ORGANIZED

By the late 18th and early 19th centuries, a kicking-and-rushing ball game was played in public schools and universities across Britain, but rules varied from place to place. In 1848, players at Cambridge University drew up football's first set of rules.

This attempt to bring order into the game had only limited success, and so in 1863 representatives of 12 clubs (including the Crusaders, No Names of Kilburn and Crystal Palace) met in London. They formed the FA, developed the laws of the game and, eight years later, set up the world's oldest surviving cup competition, the FA Cup. The first ever international, between England and Scotland, was played in 1872, and in 1888 the first football league was founded in England.

▼ This illustration shows a friendly international game between England and Scotland in 1878. Between 1873 and 1888, Scotland lost just one out of 31 international matches.

▼ The Japanese game of kemari is at least 1,500 years old. Players had to stop the ball from touching the ground by juggling and passing it with their feet. This re-enactment was held to celebrate Japan's co-hosting of the 2002 World Cup.

HIT THE NET

www.11v11.com
The website of the Association of Football Statisticians has historic photos and features on football's early history.

http://uk.women.soccerway.com
This website contains results of all leading women's football clubs and national competitions.

www.soccerballworld.com/History.htm
A thorough guide to the history and evolution of the soccer ball, from its ancient origins to the latest versions.

▼ Mana Iwabuchi of Japan pursued by Lauren Holiday in the 2015 Women's World Cup final between USA and Japan.

THE WOMEN'S GAME

Women's football struggled from the beginning against male prejudice that it was 'unladylike' for females to play the game. Interest in women's football reached its first peak after World War I thanks to the exploits of the Dick, Kerr Ladies side (see page 81). The women's game was then stifled for almost half a century following the introduction of a ban on women playing at the grounds of FA member clubs. Between 1969 and 1972, bans were lifted in a number of countries and women's football slowly began to expand. The first European Championships for women were held in 1984, while an Olympic competition was launched in 1996. More than 60 nations entered the qualifying competition for the first Women's World Cup in 1991.

FOOTBALL EXPORTS

Football spread rapidly around the globe in the late 19th century. The game was exported first by British players and then by converts from other European nations, particularly to their colonies. Football was introduced to Russia in 1887 by two English mill owners, the Charnock brothers, while resident Englishmen founded Italy's oldest league club, Genoa, six years later.

In 1885, Canada defeated the USA 1-0 in the first international match to be played in the Americas. In Argentina, British and Italian residents encouraged the formation of South America's first club, Buenos Aires, in 1865. The first league in South America was set up 28 years later.

In 1904, FIFA was founded in Paris, with seven members: Belgium, Denmark, France, Holland, Spain (represented by Madrid FC), Sweden and Switzerland. Over time, FIFA became the dominant organization in world football. In 1930, it had 45 member nations; in 1960, that figure stood at 95. In May 2012, FIFA welcomed South Sudan as its 209th member.

► W. R. Moon of Corinthians, an English amateur team, poses for a photograph in his kit. Corinthians helped to spread football by touring the world. Their 1910 trip to South America inspired the formation of the famous Brazilian side Corinthians Paulista.

THE GLOBAL GAME

FIFA is in control of world football. At continental or regional level, the game is organized by six confederations. The traditional powerhouses of international football have been Europe and South America, home to the world's richest clubs and to the winners of every World Cup. But as other regions begin to exert more influence, the global game is changing.

BALANCE OF POWER

Great advances have been made by the federations and national teams of regions outside Europe and South America. More and more national football teams have become truly competitive, thanks to the emergence of high-quality footballers in Africa, Asia, Oceania and North and Central America. Australia performed well at the 2006 World Cup (its first since 1974), narrowly losing to eventual winners Italy in the second round, and New Zealand was the only team at the 2010 World Cup not to lose a game. African nations have featured in three of the last four Olympic football finals, winning two golds and one silver. By April 2017, the continent had ten teams ranked in FIFA's top 50. There have also been strong showings by Japan, Costa Rica and the USA at recent international tournaments.

As a reflection of this, African and Asian nations have been chosen to host many tournaments, including the World Cups of 2002 (South Korea and Japan), 2010 (South Africa), 2022 (Qatar) and the Women's World Cup of 2007 (China). Additionally, Africa and Asia now enjoy more automatic places at the World Cup than ever before.

▲ Steve Mokone was the first black South African to play professionally in Europe. From the 1950s, he starred for Coventry City, Dutch side Heracles, Spain's Valencia, Marseille in France and Italy's Torino. Mokone later played in Australia and Canada.

> **FACTFILE** A European side has reached the final of all but two World Cups (1930 and 1950).

◄ Argentina line up to play Germany in the 2006 World Cup. At the time, only keeper Roberto Abbondanzieri played club football in Argentina. After the tournament, he signed for Spanish club Getafe.

CONCACAF

Confederation of North, Central American and Caribbean Association Football
www.concacaf.com
Founded: 1961
Members: 41

Mexico and the USA – traditionally the strongest CONCACAF nations – have hosted three World Cups, while smaller nations such as Costa Rica have reached the tournament. CONCACAF teams have often been invited to play in South America's Copa America competition, and the federation actually includes two South American nations, Guyana and Suriname.

UEFA

Union of European Football Associations
www.uefa.com
Founded: 1954
Members: 52

As the most powerful confederation, UEFA was awarded 13 of the 32 places at the 2014 World Cup. It runs the two largest competitions after the World Cup – the European Championships and the UEFA Champions League. Thousands of foreign footballers play in Europe, but UEFA clubs may soon be forced to include a minimum number of home-grown players in their squads.

CONMEBOL

Confederación Sudamericana de Fútbol
www.conmebol.com
Founded: 1916
Members: 10

CONMEBOL teams have won nine men's World Cup finals, whilst the Brazilian women's national team were World Cup runners-up in 2007. Argentina won the 2004 and 2008 Olympic men's finals and are rarely out of the top five of FIFA's world rankings. Domestic leagues, however, are suffering with clubs in debt and most of the continent's top players heading for Europe and elsewhere to play.

CAF
**Confédération Africaine
de Football**
www.cafonline.com
Founded: 1957
Members: 56

Africa was not awarded an automatic World Cup place until 1970, but the CAF sent six teams to the 2010 World Cup including the host nation, South Africa. While national sides continue to improve, the domestic game struggles because of a lack of finance and the movement of its best players out of Africa. In 2010, for example, more than 570 African footballers were playing in the top leagues of Europe.

AFC
Asian Football Confederation
www.the-afc.com/english/
intro.asp
Founded: 1954
Members: 47

Asian football is booming. The highly successful Asian Champions League was set up in 2002, and national leagues are now well supported. Many foreign footballers play in Asia – more than 29 Brazilians played in Japan's J-League in 2013, for example. Australia joined the AFC in 2006, but all eyes are now turning to China, which has the world's largest pool of potential players and supporters.

OFC
**Oceania Football
Confederation**
www.oceaniafootball.com
Founded: 1966
Members: 11

Football has struggled for support in Oceania. In the larger countries, it has to compete with more popular sports, while smaller nations suffer from a lack of finance, facilities and players. Australia, the OFC's biggest and most successful nation, became frustrated by the lack of an automatic World Cup place for the confederation. In January 2006 it left the OFC to join the Asian Football Confederation.

FACTFILE
Australia was the first OFC side to reach a World Cup, in 1974.

HAVE BOOTS, WILL TRAVEL

Football is flourishing all over the world, but Europe remains the most attractive destination for the world's top players. The globe's 20 richest clubs are all European, and this situation is unlikely to change for some time as a result of the huge sums of money that teams receive from television rights, advertising and qualifying for the

◀ *Givanildo Vieira de Souza, known as Hulk, stars for Brazil in a 2013 friendly game against Italy. By the age of 25, the powerful striker had played all over the world for clubs in Brazil, Japan and Portugal before being signed by Russian side, Zenit Saint Petersburg in 2012.*

Champions League. The revenue enables European clubs to pluck the best talents from around the globe. At the 2014 World Cup, only one of Uruguay, Ghana and Ivory Coast's 23-man squads played club football in their home country. In contrast, all of Russia's, 22 of England's and 20 of Italy's footballers played at home.

In the past, South American club football held on to many of its stars. Every member of Brazil's 1970 World Cup-winning side played for a club in his home country. That state of affairs has changed, with hundreds of players moving to Europe in search of higher wages and the chance to play in the most prestigious competitions, from Serie A and La Liga to the Champions League.

HIT THE NET

www.worldsoccer.com
World Soccer magazine's website focuses on global soccer and its best players, teams and competitions.

http://uk.soccerway.com
A comprehensive match website, searchable by continent, to give you the fixtures and results of all leading football competitions.

www.soccerstats.com
Get the latest football news and competition standings from around the world.

Alfredo di Stefano (in white) lashes Real Madrid's second goal past Eintracht Frankfurt keeper Egon Loy. Despite making a number of splendid saves, Loy conceded seven goals.

MADRID'S MAGNIFICENT SEVEN

Football's capacity to surprise, excite and above all entertain has rarely been better showcased than in the final of the fifth European Cup, in 1960. Real Madrid, winners of the first four competitions, met Eintracht Frankfurt in front of a record crowd of more than 130,000 at Scotland's Hampden Park. Eintracht took an early lead. Was Real's reign as the undoubted masters of Europe about to end? The answer was an emphatic no. Led by Hungarian genius Ferenc Puskas and Argentinian all-rounder Alfredo di Stefano, the

Spanish side put on a dazzling display of attacking football. In an electrifying 45 minutes, Real went from 1-0 down to 6-1 up, courtesy of goals by both Puskas and di Stefano. But the enterprising German side were just as committed to attack. They fought back, scoring two goals and hitting the woodwork twice, while Real countered with their seventh and di Stefano's third goal to eventually triumph 7-3. No one who witnessed the game would ever forget the spectacle of Europe's finest club side playing at the peak of its skills.

BASIC SKILLS

In the words of former Liverpool manager Bill Shankly, 'Football is a simple game based on the giving and taking of passes, on controlling the ball and on making yourself available to receive a pass.' Shankly's words highlight the most fundamental skills in football.

BALL CONTROL

The world's top players, such as Cristiano Ronaldo and Lionel Messi, appear to control the ball effortlessly. Their easy command and movement of the ball masks thousands of hours of practice and training, often from a very early age. As children, many great footballers spent long hours playing games with a tennis ball, crumpled ball of paper or a battered piece of fruit.

Players can control the ball with any part of their body except for their hands and arms. Cushioning is a technique in which a player uses a part of the body to slow down a moving ball and then bring it under control with his or her feet. High balls can be cushioned using the chest, thigh or a gentle header to kill the ball's speed and bring it down. For a low, incoming ball, the foot is preferred – either the inside of the boot or its instep (where the laces are). A ball that is rolling across the pitch can be stopped with the sole of the foot – a technique known as trapping.

▲ *French female footballers practise their close control skills by keeping the ball up using their head and feet. Good ball control only comes with hundreds of hours of practice.*

▶ *David Beckham leans back to perform a chest cushion during a Real Madrid training session. A good chest cushion sees the ball drop at the feet of the player, who can then pass, run or shoot.*

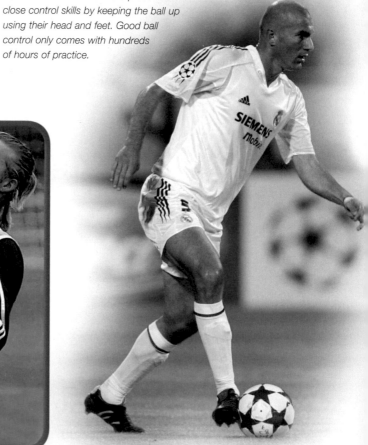

▲ *French legend Zinedine Zidane uses the side of his foot to control the ball during a Champions League match against Bayer Leverkusen.*

◀ *An instep cushion is used to control a ball arriving front-on. Here, the player meets the ball with the laces of his boot and instantly pulls back his foot, killing the pace of the ball.*

SHIELDING AND OBSTRUCTION

When footballers have the ball at their feet, they are said to be in possession and have a number of options. These include: running with the ball; dribbling with the ball close to the feet; passing; shooting; and shielding the ball. Shielding or screening involves a player putting his or her body between the ball and an opponent to prevent the other player from gaining possession. This gives the shielding player crucial time to decide on the next move, which may be a pass backwards to a team-mate or a sharp turn and an attempt to play the ball round the opponent. Shielding players have to be careful not to hold, push or back into the other player. They must also keep the ball close by and under control, otherwise the referee may award an indirect free kick for obstruction (in which a player unfairly blocks an opponent's path to the ball). An obstruction usually occurs when a player steps into the path of an opponent when the ball is several metres away.

◀ *Sergiy Nazarenko of Ukrainian side Dnipro Dnipropetrovsk shields the ball from FC Utrecht's Etienne Shew-Atjon during a 2004–05 UEFA Cup match.*

▼ *Australia's Nick Carle challenges Japan's Uchida Atsuto for the ball.*

▶ *Pavel Nedved of Juventus hits a long instep drive pass during a Serie A match against Messina.*

PASS MASTERS

Passes can be made with a thrust of the chest or with a carefully directed header. Usually, however, they are made with one of three parts of the boot – the outside, the instep or the inside. The inside or sidefoot pass is the most common and accurate pass, allowing players to stroke the ball around with a high level of precision. Some players attempt as many as 60 or 70 passes in a game, most of which are sidefoot passes. At the 2014 World Cup Italy's Daniele De Rossi made an average of 106 passes per game.

For longer passes, players tend to use the instep. This allows them to propel the ball with force. The instep can also be used for lofted drives that send the ball into the air as a cross or a clearance, as well as to stab down on the back of the ball. This makes the ball rise up at a steep angle, known as a chip. A pass's weight – the strength with which it is hit – is as important as accuracy for the pass to be successfully completed. At Euro 2016, strong passers such as Germans Toni Kroos and Mesut Özil and Spain's Andrés Iniesta made hundreds of passes with over 90 per cent success.

▶ *Brek Shea plays an accurate sidefoot pass for his MLS side, FC Dallas, with his foot striking through the middle of the ball. Shea moved on to Stoke City and Orlando before joining Vancouver Whitecaps in 2017.*

MOVEMENT AND SPACE

Football is a dynamic, fast-moving sport. Throughout a game, pockets of space open and close all over the pitch. A player who has an awareness of where space exists, or where it will shortly open up, is a great asset to a team. Equally valuable is the ability to move into that space to receive a pass. The more space a player is in, the more time he or she usually has to receive the ball, control it and attack with it.

SPOTTING AND CREATING SPACE

The ball can zip around a pitch far more quickly than even the fastest of players. Good footballers make the ball do the work, moving it around with quick, accurate passes. Vision is the priceless ability to spot a pass, space or goalscoring opportunity that other players do not see, or before they do. Players with good vision look to move into space, timing their run to give a team-mate who has the ball a chance of making a pass that cannot be intercepted by an opponent. Once the ball has left the passer's control, he or she often moves into a position to receive a return pass. All players, not just midfielders and attackers, must be capable of passing well and moving into space to receive passes in return.

Players can create space for themselves or for team-mates through quick, agile movement and the use of feints or dummies,

► *Mesut Özil picks a pass to play to a Real Madrid team-mate. Top players such as Özil play with their head up, scouring the pitch for team-mates' moves and runs. Özil moved to Arsenal in 2013.*

with which they attempt to fool a nearby opponent into thinking they are moving one way, before sprinting off in another direction. World-class players such as Mesut Özil, Lionel Messi and Andrés Iniesta are particularly skilled at outwitting an opponent in this way to find space.

▲ *Dutch winger Arjen Robben (right) attempts to go round the outside of Portugal's Miguel in the semi-final of Euro 2004.*

◄ *A wall pass (also known as a one-two pass) is a classic way to cut out an opposition player. It involves two passes that must be hit quickly and accurately, with the first passer running on to collect the return ball.*

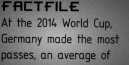

FACTFILE
At the 2014 World Cup, Germany made the most passes, an average of 106 passes per game.

▲ *Making space can be crucial to winning the ball at a throw-in. Here, one player makes a decoy run towards the thrower, dragging a defender with him and creating space in which a team-mate can collect the ball.*

OFFSIDE

Teams have to stay aware of Law 11, the offside law, throughout a match. In 1847, under the rules of Eton College, being offside was known as 'sneaking'. A player was caught sneaking when there were three or fewer opposition players between him and the goal at the moment a team-mate passed the ball forwards. The rule has been tinkered with over the years. The most notable change came in 1925, when the number of players between the attacker and the goal was reduced from three to two. The result was a goal avalanche, as defences struggled to cope with the rule change and attackers took advantage. In the English leagues, for example, 1,673 more goals were scored in the 1925–26 season than under the old law in the previous year.

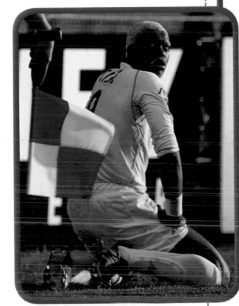

▲ *French striker Djibril Cissé looks ruefully at the referee's assistant after being signalled offside in a French league match.*

Today, a player is offside if, at the moment the ball is played, he or she is in the opposition half and is nearer the opponent's goal line than both the ball and the second-from last opponent. That opponent can be an outfield player or the goalkeeper. Players cannot be offside in their own half or if they receive the ball directly from a goal kick, throw-in or corner.

Being in an offside position is not always an offence. Referees must judge whether the player in an offside position is involved in active play, moves towards the ball or does anything to make it harder for an opponent to play the ball. This tests an official's judgement to the limit. Is a player offside but a long way from the ball involved in 'active play'? Perhaps he or she is drawing defenders out as markers. If a referee does stop the game, an indirect free kick is awarded to the opposing team where the player was judged offside.

▲ *Here, the player at the top left of the picture is in an offside position when the ball is struck. The referee decides that he is not interfering with play, however, and awards the goal.*

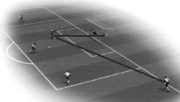

▲ *You cannot be offside if you are behind the ball when it is played. This scorer receives the ball from a team-mate who is ahead of him, so he is onside and the goal is given.*

HIT THE NET

www.dynamic-thought.com/OffsideClickette.html
Diagrams and animations that fully explain the offside law.

www.fifa.com/development/education-and-technical/referees/laws-of-the-game.html
View the latest laws of the game as approved by FIFA or download them in PDF format.

www.asktheref.com
A site for budding referees – learn more about the laws of the game and the jobs of football officials.

www.futsalplanet.com
A website dedicated to futsal, with tournament news and results as well as links to the laws of the game.

SMALL-SIDED GAMES

In many countries, children under the age of 11 play matches that feature six, seven or eight players per team. These small-sided games give young footballers an invaluable chance to see more of the ball and improve their control, passing and movement. Futsal is FIFA's official five-a-side game. A match lasts for 40 minutes (two halves of 20 minutes) and is played on a pitch the size of a basketball court, without surrounding boards or walls. Futsal was devised by a Uruguayan, Juan Carlos Ceriani, in 1930. The game flourished and developed throughout South America, with the first international competition – the South American Cup – taking place in 1965. The first futsal World Championship took place in the Netherlands in 1989. Held in Colombia, the 2016 Futsal World Cup was won by Argentina, who defeated Russia 5-4 in the final.

▲ *Spain and Brazil battle it out in the final of the 2004 Futsal World Championship, held in Taipei, Taiwan. Spain won the 40-match tournament, beating the Brazilians 5-4 in a penalty shootout after a 2-2 draw.*

OFFICIALS

Frequently abused by players, managers and supporters, referees are football's guardians and the enforcers of its laws. Their job is to impose order on a match and prevent intimidation, injury and cheating.

THE REFEREE'S ROLE

Referees perform a surprisingly large number of tasks before and after a match. These include checking the goals, nets and balls and deciding whether the pitch and weather conditions are suitable for the game to go ahead. Afterwards, they write a report containing details of disciplinary actions and other important incidents. On the pitch, the referee runs the game. His or her duties range from adding on time because of injuries, other stoppages and time-wasting, to deciding whether the ball is in or out of play or has crossed the goal line. If a player commits a foul or breaks a law, referees must stop play and order a restart, such as a drop ball or a free kick. They can caution players and team officials, and even abandon a match if weather, crowd trouble or another factor makes the game unplayable. Referees have to follow the laws of the game, but they have a certain amount of freedom to interpret aspects of the rules as they wish. For example, if a player is fouled when his or her side is in a promising position, a referee may let the match continue, playing the advantage rule to keep the game flowing.

ASSISTANTS AND THE FOURTH OFFICIAL

A referee relies on his or her assistants as extra pairs of eyes. Referee's assistants indicate when the ball goes out of play and whether a goal kick, corner or throw-in should be awarded. They also use flag signals to point out that a substitution has been requested, a player is offside or whether an offence has taken place out of the view of the referee. A referee can consult with an assistant if he or she was closer to the action, but it is up to the referee to make the final decision. In some competitions, a fourth official carries out duties before and after a match and also performs touchline tasks. These include helping with substitutions and displaying the amount of time added on at the end of a game for stoppages.

> **FACTFILE** In 1998, English referee Martin Sylvester sent himself off after punching a player during a match in the Andover and District Sunday League.

▲ The fourth official checks the boot studs of Paraguayan substitute Nelson Vera in a World Youth Championship match against Uruguay.

▼ Managers and team officials can be cautioned or sent off if they use abusive language or do not behave responsibly. Here, Martin O'Neill argues with UEFA Cup officials as he is sent off during a match.

▲ Referee Stephane Lannoy shows Mario Balotelli a yellow card after the Italian striker took his shirt off to celebrate a goal he scored at Euro 2012.

◄ Early in a game, a good referee talks to players to calm them down or issues verbal warnings rather than yellow and red cards. Here, Nicole Petignat tries to soothe AIK Solna's Krister Nordin in the first UEFA Cup game to be refereed by a woman, in 2003.

TOP-FLIGHT PRESSURES

Thousands of amateur referees give up their weekends and evenings for free, purely to give something back to the game they adore. In contrast, officials in charge of major championship matches are minor celebrities who are paid significant sums. This is a reflection of the importance of their job. Top referees have their performances assessed, attend training seminars, undergo regular medical checks and are tested for fitness. A referee may run between 9.5 and 11.5km during a match (even further if extra time occurs) and often has to sprint to keep up with play. Referees work in a harsh, unforgiving climate, in which footage from multiple cameras and slow-motion television replays are broadcast over and over again, highlighting each poor decision. However, the very technology that has put referees under the spotlight is now coming to their aid with goal-line technology being adopted, for example, the English Premier League used this for the first time in 2013.

▲ Referee Horacio Elizondo shows the red card to France's Zinedine Zidane during the 2006 World Cup final. The midfielder was sent off for headbutting Italian defender Marco Materazzi in the chest during extra time.

CAUTION

A player is shown a yellow card if he or she:

- is guilty of unsporting behaviour, such as simulation;
- shows dissent by word or action;
- persistently breaks the rules, by making repeated foul tackles for example;
- delays the restart of play;
- fails to stand at the required distance at a corner kick or free kick;
- enters or leaves the field of play without the referee's permission.

A player is sent off if he or she receives two yellow cards or one red card. Red-card offences include a very dangerous tackle, spitting and stopping a goal with a deliberate handball.

SIMULATION

Looking out for contact in the penalty area during a fast-moving attack is especially difficult for an official. In the modern game, attackers appear to fall to the ground under the slightest pressure from an opponent. Referees have to judge if a foul was committed or whether the attacker was guilty of 'simulation'. Many people think that simulation is only about diving without contact in order to win a free kick or a penalty. It is actually defined as pretending to be fouled in any way to gain an advantage. At the 2002 World Cup, Rivaldo was guilty of a simulation that led to Turkey's Hakan Ünsal being sent off. In a 2009 game in Colombia, Carmelo Valencia simulated a foul to get opposing goalkeeper Agustín Julio sent off. Valencia later received a one-game ban. In 2011, the MLS began to use match video reviews to punish simulating players with fines and bans. Other leagues may now do the same.

▲ AC Milan midfielder Andrea Pirlo battles for the ball with Deportivo La Coruña's Juan Carlos Valerón. The referee has to decide in a split second if a foul was committed and, if so, whether it is serious enough for a booking or a sending off.

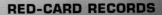

RED-CARD RECORDS

FASTEST IN A TOP LEAGUE
Ten seconds – Giuseppe Lorenzo, Serie A Bologna v Parma, 1990

FASTEST IN THE WORLD CUP
55 seconds – José Batista, Uruguay v Scotland, 1986

MOST IN ONE MATCH
36 – Claypole v Victoriano Arenas (Argentina), 2011

DEFENDING

Compared to strikers or creative midfielders, defenders are rarely praised as match-winners. Yet the foundation of every successful team is a composed, secure defence. Defending consists of a range of individual skills allied to good teamwork and understanding between players so that they defend as a unit. Defenders require strength and excellent heading and tackling skills, along with intense concentration, quick reactions and bravery. But, in truth, all players must defend if their side is to remain competitive in a match.

▼ After tracking Bayern Munich's Arjen Robben (right), Real Madrid's Adriano times his tackle to rob his opponent of the ball. In situations like this, team-mates look to pounce on the ball to gain possession.

▲ Portugal's Nuno Gomes (left) and Russia's Alexei Bugaev challenge for the ball. Forceful tackles that target the ball, not the player, are a key part of defending.

TRACKING AND TACKLING

The two keys to defending well are denying the opposition the chance to score and winning the ball back. As soon as an opponent gets the ball, defenders try to get between the ball and their goal and close down space. Defenders spend much of a game tracking opponents as they make runs and closing down the player with the ball to delay his or her progress. This is called jockeying. The aim is to slow down an attack until the defending side is in a stronger position. The defender tries to shepherd the attacker into a weaker position, such as near the sideline where there is little support. When a defender has cover from nearby team-mates, he or she may make a tackle. The defender should stay on his or her feet in order to gain possession.

► This attacker has spotted a weak pass by an opponent and reacts quickly to make an interception. Sometimes, attackers drop back to help their team defend.

FALLING FOUL OF THE LAW

Many of football's laws, such as obstruction, apply to defenders. A jockeying defender must be careful not to commit a foul, such as pushing, holding or shirt-pulling. A poorly timed tackle may result in a foul. Tackles from behind are especially risky, often leading to a yellow or red card if the defender makes contact with the attacker. A professional foul is a deliberate foul made to deny an attacking side a clear goalscoring chance. Two of the most common types are using the hands or arms to stop a goalbound ball and bringing down an attacker with the ball when he or she has a clear path to goal. Both should result in a sending off.

▲ A supporting defender can step in to help if his team-mate is beaten. Here, Pablo Zabaleta (right) challenges Chelsea's Fernando Torres for the ball after his Manchester City team-mate, Vincent Kompany, has been brushed aside.

CLEAN SHEETS

Goalkeepers and defenders are especially proud of a clean sheet – a game in which their side does not concede a goal. Clean sheets are usually credited to goalkeepers, but in truth they depend on a solid defence as well as midfielders and strikers who are willing to chase, harry, track and tackle. Italy has a reputation for producing some of the world's finest defenders. Between 1972 and the 1974 World Cup, the Italian defence helped keeper Dino Zoff to play 1,142 minutes – more than 12 matches – without conceding a goal. The run was finally ended by Haiti. In 2009, Edwin van der Sar set an English record of 1,311 minutes unbeaten in goal for Manchester United. The world record in professional football is held by Brazil's Geraldo Pereira de Matos Filho, better known as Mazaropi. Playing for Vasco da Gama in 1977–78, he did not concede a goal for over 20 games, a total of 1,816 minutes.

FACTFILE
Juventus went unbeaten in the competitive Serie A league during the 38-game 2011–12 season.

▶ Tamas Priskin of Hungarian club, Gyor, makes a defensive header above Ferencvaros' Zolta Gera.

DEFENSIVE FORTRESS

During periods of open play, defending teams mark opponents man-to-man or with a zonal system (see page 62). At corners and free kicks from a wide position, they tend to mark man-to-man. A team may also try to catch out attackers by playing an offside trap (see page 62). Communication between defenders is crucial to prevent attackers getting free and into space to score. Certain teams equipped with highly skilled defenders who work well together have been able to squeeze the life out of opposition attacks. The AC Milan side of 1992–93, for example, scored 26 goals and conceded only two during their entire nine-game Champions League campaign. In England, Chelsea hold the record for conceding the fewest goals in a season (2004–05) – just 15 goals in 38 matches.

▲ Real Madrid's Ivan Helguera and David Beckham hurl themselves bravely into the path of the ball to block a fierce shot from Asier del Horno of Athletic Bilbao.

LONGEST UNBEATEN LEAGUE RUNS (IN GAMES)

108	ASEC Abidjan (Ivory Coast), 1989–94
104	Steaua Bucharest (Romania), 1986–89
88	Lincoln FC (Gibraltar), 2009–14
85	Esperance (Tunisia), 1997–2001
71	Al-Ahly (Egypt), 2004–07
63	Sheriff Tiraspol (Moldova), 2006–08
62	Celtic (Scotland), 1915–17
61	Levadia Tallinn (Estonia), 2008–09
60	Union Saint-Gilloise (Belgium), 1933–35
59	Boca Juniors (Argentina), 1924–27
	Pyunik Yerevan (Armenia), 2002–04
58	AC Milan (Italy), 1991–93
	Olympiakos (Greece), 1972–74
	Skonto Riga (Latvia), 1993–96
56	Benfica (Portugal), 1976–78
	Peñarol (Uruguay), 1966–69

GOALKEEPING

Goalkeepers are a breed apart. They have a different role to their team-mates and even look a little different, as they must wear a shirt that distinguishes them from other players and officials. The crucial last line of defence, keepers can be forgotten when things are going well, but singled out for abuse when they make a mistake that leads to a goal. Goalkeepers can also be match-winners thanks to their saves and decisions, their agility and bravery.

▲ *Goalkeeper Shay Given stretches to make a diving save. The veteran has made 125 international appearances for the Republic of Ireland.*

◄ *At the 2003 Women's World Cup, Norway's Bente Nordby clears a dangerous ball by punching it firmly away from goal.*

KEEPING CONTROL

Goalkeepers are allowed to control the ball with their hands and arms, but otherwise they must obey most of the same rules as outfield players. Until 1912, keepers could handle the ball anywhere in their own half, but now handling is restricted to their penalty area, with several key exceptions. Goalkeepers cannot handle the ball:

- after releasing it and without it touching another player;
- after receiving it directly from a throw-in;
- if it has been deliberately kicked to them by a team-mate.

If a goalkeeper handles the ball in any of these situations or if the referee judges that the keeper is time-wasting with the ball in hand (known as the six-second rule), an indirect free kick is awarded. This can be dangerously close to the goal. In the 1990s, a law was passed to reduce time-wasting and speed up play. It banned keepers from controlling a ball from a throw-in or backpass with their arms or hands.

In the past, goalkeepers could be barged into heavily, but today they are well protected by referees. Even so, they have to be brave to dive at an opponent's feet, risking injury. If keepers foul or bring down an attacker, they may give away a penalty and even be sent off if the referee decides that a professional foul has been committed.

▲ *Czech goalkeeper Petr Cech gathers the ball cleanly at the feet of Manchester City defender Aleksandar Kolarov.*

A KEEPER'S SKILLS

To achieve a clean sheet, goalkeepers need more than supreme agility and the talent to make diving saves. Top keepers train hard to improve their handling skills, learning to take the ball at different heights and from different angles. They must be able to stay alert for the entire game. Many minutes can go by before, suddenly, they are called into action. Keepers need good decision-making skills, too, as a cross or shot may call for them to choose whether to try to hold the ball in a save, punch it away or tip it over the bar or round a post. Goalkeepers are in a unique position to see opposition attacks developing, and they must communicate instructions to their team-mates. They line up walls at free kicks and command their goal area, urging defenders to pick up unmarked opponents. A defence and keeper that communicate well can be a formidable unit.

▶ *Italian keeper Gianluigi Buffon instructs his defenders. Clear, decisive communication between a keeper and his or her outfield team-mates can snuff out many opposition attacks.*

DEFENCE INTO ATTACK

With the ball in hand, keepers have several ways in which they can move the ball to a team-mate or up the pitch (known as distribution). They can roll it out on the floor, looking for options to kick the ball; they can kick it straight from their hand; or they can throw the ball. Keepers launch the ball from their hand into the opposition half by using their boot instep to strike it on the volley or half volley. Sometimes, keepers aim their kick for a tall winger or wide midfielder who is close to the sideline. This move is often rehearsed on the training ground. Keepers can bowl the ball out underarm, usually to a nearby team-mate, or they can use a more powerful sidearm or overarm motion for maximum distance. A third option, the javelin throw, is often the quickest way to get the ball moving. Fast, accurate distribution from the keeper can be vital in turning defence into a rapid breakaway attack.

HIT THE NET

www.goalkeepersaredifferent.com
A fabulous website that is dedicated solely to keepers and is packed with quirky facts.

www.fourfourtwo.com/performance/goalkeepers
A great collection of videos showing tips and training from top professional goalkeepers.

www.jbgoalkeeping.com
An impressive coaching website, with short online videos, covering all aspects of the keeper's game.

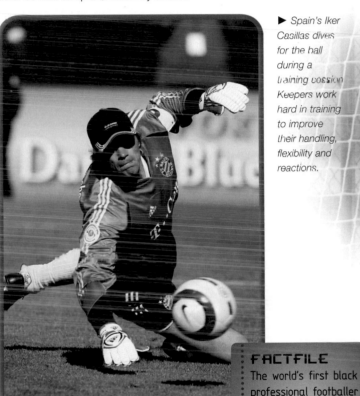

▲ Germany's Oliver Kahn goes to make a save. In 2002, Kahn was FIFA's Goalkeeper of the World Cup. During the following league season with Bayern Munich, he set a Bundesliga record of 737 minutes without conceding a goal.

▶ Spain's Iker Casillas dives for the ball during a training session. Keepers work hard in training to improve their handling, flexibility and reactions.

FACTFILE
The world's first black professional footballer was a goalkeeper. Born in the Gold Coast (now Ghana), Arthur Wharton turned out in 1889 for Rotherham United in the English league.

▶ In a one-on-one situation, many keepers come off their line to narrow the angle – reducing how much of the goal the attacker can see. They stay upright for as long as possible to increase the chance of the shot striking them.

GOALSCORING KEEPERS

In 1882, goalkeeper James McAulay was pressed into service as a centre-forward and scored in Scotland's 5-0 defeat of Wales. Since then, many keepers have scored goals for their club or country. Some goals have been scored from long goal kicks that have caught out a defence or by goalkeepers running into the opposition's penalty area in the dying seconds of a game. Others have come from spot kicks in a penalty shootout (see page 31). A well-taken penalty by Portuguese keeper Ricardo knocked England out of Euro 2004, for example. A few keepers have become legends for their goalscoring feats from regular penalties and free kicks. The German Hans-Jörg Butt scored 28 goals, while Paraguay's José Luis Chilavert struck 62 times. This staggering tally was more than doubled during the remarkable career of Rogério Ceni. He scored 131 goals during his career for Brazilian club, São Paulo. His 100th came in 2011 with a free kick struck from outside the penalty area.

ATTACKING

As soon as a team gains possession of the ball, with time and in space, its players' thoughts turn to attack. There are many ways in which a team can launch an attack, from a fast drive into space by a player who is sprinting forwards and pushing the ball ahead, to a slow, probing attack in which many players keep the ball securely in possession and look for an opening.

BEATING OFFSIDE TRAPS

Some teams play an offside trap (see page 62), in which defenders move up in a straight line to catch opponents offside. Beating an offside trap takes cunning, skill and awareness. A perfectly weighted through pass can unlock the trap if the ball is collected by a player who stays onside until the moment the ball moves ahead of him or her. A long diagonal pass that switches play forwards and across the pitch may also work. The receiver makes a run from a deep position, staying onside until the ball moves ahead, then collects the ball behind the defence. Individual brilliance – such as dribbling or playing a short 'push and go' pass – can also beat some offside traps.

▲ *Ludovic Giuly of Barcelona threads an accurate through pass between Shakhtar Donetsk defenders Anatoliy Tymoschuk and Mariusz Lewandowski in a UEFA Champions League game.*

◀ *France's Franck Ribéry dribbles between Dutch defender Khalid Boulahrouz and forward Robin van Persie during a Euro 2008 group match. Great teamwork and accurate counter-attacking saw the Dutch side win 4-1.*

▲ *A 'push and go' pass can beat a lone defender or an offside trap. The attacker pushes the ball past the defender and then sprints to collect it.*

TEAM ATTACKS

Many attacks rely on two or more team-mates working together to create a promising position. The wall pass (see page 18), for example, is a good way of propelling the ball past a defender with two quick movements. Attacking players also make decoy runs that draw defenders in one direction, creating space for another attacker to run into. Using the full width of the pitch can be vital to the success of an attack. Full-backs, wing-backs or wingers who are in space near the sideline may join an attack and make an overlapping run down the line. Receiving the ball, they may be able to head further forwards to put in a cross or cut infield and move towards goal. An overload is a situation in which the attacking side has more players in the attacking third of the pitch than the defending team. Classic ways of creating an overload are through a counter-attack – in which one side's attack breaks down and the opposition launches a rapid, direct attack – and an accurate long pass that is received by an attacker who is supported by team-mates, with only an isolated defender to beat.

SET PIECES

Set pieces are often planned in training. They are attacking moves made from a restart such as a free kick, corner or throw-in. If a team has a player who can throw the ball a long way, it may treat a throw-in that is level with the penalty area as if it were a corner. Often, a target player just inside the penalty area will attempt to flick the throw into the goal area. Mostly, set pieces are planned from corners and attacking free kicks (see page 30). At a corner, a team's tallest players or its best headers of the ball move up, usually from defence, to join strikers and attacking midfielders in the penalty area. Corners are sometimes played short to catch the defending team off guard, but usually they are whipped into the goal area. The attacking side looks for a header or shot on goal or a flick-on to a team-mate.

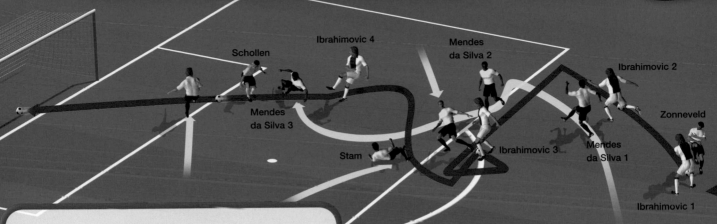

Schollen
Ibrahimovic 4
Mendes da Silva 2
Ibrahimovic 2
Zonneveld
Mendes da Silva 3
Stam
Ibrahimovic 3
Mendes da Silva 1
Ibrahimovic 1

MATCH ACTION

Swedish international Zlatan Ibrahimovic moved from Ajax to Juventus for £10.81 million in late August 2004, but a week earlier he had given the Ajax fans a solo goal to savour. In a Dutch league game against NAC Breda, Ibrahimovic received a pass with his back to goal, defender David Mendes da Silva on his back and another Breda player, Mike Zonneveld, close by. Winning a tackle with Zonneveld, Ibrahimovic twisted past da Silva and headed goalwards. Weaving his way to the edge of the penalty area, Ibrahimovic's options looked limited with four defenders around him. Yet with supreme balance and a series of feints and turns, he avoided the lunging tackle of Ronnie Stam. At the very last moment, when a shot with his right foot looked likely, Ibrahimovic switched the ball to his left foot to slide a shot past goalkeeper Davy Schollen. Ajax won the game 6-2.

▼ *Ghana's Stephen Appiah (left) attempts to twist and turn sharply past Zimbabwean defender Cephas Chimedza in the African Cup of Nations. Dummy movements, stepovers and sharp turns are all ways of wrong-footing a defender.*

MATCH MAGICIANS

Some attacks are inspired by a piece of individual skill, trickery and brilliance. A player may be able to break free from a defence with a sudden change of pace and direction or a trick move such as the Cruyff turn or a dragback. Some players can simply outpace a defence, bursting through to score. Dribbling – jinking and moving with the ball under close control to beat defenders – is one of the most exciting sights on a football pitch. Stanley Matthews, Maradona and Garrincha were all electrifying dribblers, while today's dribbling superstars include Gareth Bale, Cristiano Ronaldo, Lionel Messi and Ousmane Dembélé. Weaving, high-speed dribblers can sometimes open up a game by themselves. They strike fear into defenders who know that one false move or a poorly timed challenge will allow the dribbler to go past or perhaps give away a free kick or penalty.

▲ *An unexpected piece of brilliance can open up a defence or result in a goal. Here, whilst playing for Sevilla, Jesus Navas unleashes an overhead kick against Barcelona. In 2013, he moved to Manchester City for £14.9 million.*

GOALSCORING

Players who score goals regularly are the most valuable of all footballers. But scoring is not just reserved for the strikers in a side. A successful team needs its midfielders to contribute a number of goals each season, while tall defenders who are experts at heading often score five or six goals per season from set pieces. For out-and-out strikers, goals are what they play for and are judged on. As Argentinian striker Gabriel Batistuta once said, 'Goals are like bread. I need them to live.'

THE GOALSCORER'S ART

Pace, power, accuracy, confidence and a deadly eye for a chance are just some of the qualities required to be a top goalscorer. Some skills can be honed in training – close ball control or swerving a shot, for example. Other qualities, such as confidence and vision, are harder to master. Football has got quicker at the highest level and most strikers need great pace to break past increasingly mobile defenders or into space to receive the ball before anyone else. Strength to hold off a challenge can be an asset, too. Some strikers, however, rely more on wits, fast reactions and ball skills to dribble through a crowded penalty area. Others are taller, stronger players who can score with towering headers or blasted shots. Most crucially of all, strikers have to be able to spot a goal chance and take it well. They need to react instinctively, using their vision to time runs into a scoring position. Once on the ball, they rarely have long to shoot. In an instant, strikers have to weigh up their options, know where the goal, defenders and keeper are, and hit a shot with enough pace, bend or accuracy to beat the goalkeeper.

FACTFILE In 1998, Atlético Mineiro's Edmilson Ferreira celebrated a goal by eating a carrot in front of the fans of rival Brazilian team America MG. His actions caused crowd trouble and incensed America's players, one of whom was later sent off for a scything foul on Ferreira.

OWN GOALS

An own goal is technically any goal in which the last person to touch the ball before it crossed the line was a player on the defending team. In practice, however, an own goal is awarded not only when the ball has been deflected, but also when a defending player has made a genuine error or caused a major change in the course of the ball. The history of professional football is littered with outrageous own goals. Among the most common are goalkeeping errors, skewed defensive clearances that are sliced into the net, and misdirected headers. A handful of players have scored two own goals in the same game, such as Georgia's Kakhaber 'Kakha' Kaladze in a 2010 World Cup match versus Italy, and Stoke City's Jon Walters in a 2013 Premier League game against Chelsea.

◄ *Manchester United's Wayne Rooney hits a volley to score against Liverpool in an English Premier League match. His thunderous shot is ideal for striking at goal from outside the penalty area.*

FACTFILE
The world record for own goals in one game is a staggering 149! In the last match of the 2002 Madagascan league season, against champions AS Adema, Stade Olympique l'Emryne repeatedly scored own goals from the kick-off in protest at a refereeing decision in their previous game.

► *Germany's Miroslav Klose scored five goals in the 2006 World Cup and is the competition's all-time record holder with 16 goals in four tournaments.*

▲ When a goalscoring chance comes, strikers need poise and accuracy to put it away. Here, Fernando Torres scores the winning goal of the Euro 2008 final, placing the ball past the German goalkeeper, Jens Lehmann.

▶ Fabian Espindola (left) roars with joy after scoring for Real Salt Lake against LA Galaxy in 2011. The Argentinean scored more than 30 goals for Real Salt Lake before moving in 2013 to New York Red Bulls.

FACTFILE Nigerian international Celestine Babayaro scored on his debut for Chelsea in a 1997 pre-season match against Stevenage Borough. By celebrating with a somersault, however, Babayaro broke his leg.

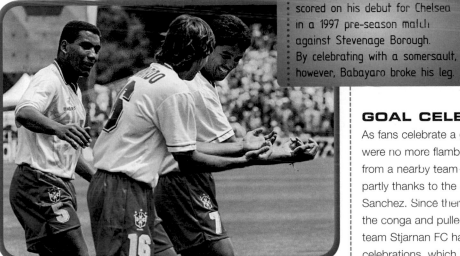

▲ Brazil's Mauro Silva (left), Leonardo (centre) and Bebeto pretend to rock babies at the 1994 World Cup. The celebration – during a 3-0 victory against Cameroon – was in honour of striker Bebeto's newborn son.

GOALSCORING RECORDS

ALL-TIME LEADING GOALSCORERS
Artur Friedenreich (Brazil)
1,329 goals (1909-39)

Pelé (Brazil)
1,281 goals (1956-77)

MOST INTERNATIONAL GOALS (MEN)
109 – Ali Daei (Iran), 1993-2006

MOST INTERNATIONAL GOALS (WOMEN)
184 – Abby Wambach (USA), 2001-15

MOST GOALS IN ONE INTERNATIONAL MATCH
13 – Archie Thompson (Australia), 2001

FASTEST INTERNATIONAL GOAL
8 seconds – Davide Gualtieri (San Marino) against England, 1993

FASTEST INTERNATIONAL HAT-TRICK
Inside 3½ minutes – Willie Hall (England), 1938

MOST HAT-TRICKS IN CONSECUTIVE MATCHES
4 – Masashi Nakayama (Japan) for Jubilo Iwata, 1998

FASTEST GOAL
2 seconds – Vuk Bakic (Serbia) for GSP Polet, 2012

FASTEST OWN GOAL
8 seconds – Pat Kruse (England), playing for Torquay United, 1977

GOAL CELEBRATIONS

As fans celebrate a goal, so do players. For many years, celebrations were no more flamboyant than a simple punch of the air and a hug from a nearby team-mate. That all changed in the 1980s and 1990s, partly thanks to the acrobatic backflips of Mexican striker Hugo Sanchez. Since then, players have rocked imaginary babies, danced the conga and pulled off spectacular gymnastic moves. Icelandic team Stjarnan FC have gained fame for their elaborate team celebrations, which include all the team members pretending to row a boat and reel in a player acting as a fish. This performance clocked up over a million views on YouTube in 2011. Referees can penalize teams for time-wasting or removing shirts during such celebrations.

FREE KICKS AND PENALTIES

Referees award a free kick when a player breaks one of the laws of the game. Common free-kick offences are mistimed tackles, shirt-pulling, obstruction and offside. There are two types of free kick – indirect, which cannot be scored from without a second player touching the ball, and direct, which can be scored from directly and is awarded for more serious fouls. If a direct free-kick offence is committed by the defending team inside its penalty area, the referee may award a penalty.

FREE KICKS

Both types of free kick are taken from where the foul or offence was committed, although a rule change means that in some competitions the referee can move a kick 9m closer to goal if the other team wastes time or shows dissent. Opposition players must move at least 9m away from the ball, giving the team taking the kick valuable possession in space and with time. Some free kicks are taken quickly to get the ball moving in the middle of the field. Wide free kicks are often crossed with pace towards the goal area.

Attacking free kicks engage the two teams in a battle of wits. Players on the defending side mark attackers in the penalty area and form a defensive wall to block a direct shot. The kick taker may pass to a team-mate in space or try to hit a cross or shot past the wall. Some free kick specialists rely on powerful and direct strikes, while others – such as Dimitri Payet, Hakan Calhanoglu and Cristiano Ronaldo – are famous for the extreme bend they put on the ball.

▲ Lionel Messi takes a free kick during a 2013 Champions League match between Barcelona and AC Milan. He strikes across the back of the ball to make it swerve round the defensive wall and into the corner of the goal.

◄ Manchester United's Wayne Rooney curls a free kick towards the penalty area.

THE KICK OF DEATH

Originally nicknamed the 'kick of death', the penalty kick was introduced in 1891. It has created more controversy than any other aspect of the game. The reason is simple. A penalty is an outstanding opportunity to score, as the taker is one-on-one with the goalkeeper and all the other players are outside the penalty area. In certain situations, the referee can order the kick to be retaken – for example, if the taker misses but a defender entered the area before the kick. Penalty takers must hit the ball forwards and cannot make contact with the ball again until it has touched another player. Some penalty takers favour accuracy over power, aiming the ball low into the corner of the goal; others blast the ball. For the keeper, trying to figure out where the ball will go is a guessing game.

PENALTY SHOOTOUTS

Tense and nailbiting, a penalty shootout is guaranteed to bring fans to the edge of their seats. Professional football's first shootout took place in England in 1970. In the semi-final of the Watney Mann Invitational Cup, lowly Hull City held a full-strength Manchester United team to a 1-1 draw. In the shootout that followed, Manchester United's Denis Law became the first player to miss a shootout spot kick, but his side ended up 4-3 winners. The first shootout in a major tournament was in the 1972 Asian Nations Cup, when South Korea beat Thailand in the semi-final. Germany lost the first European Championships shootout to Czechoslovakia in 1976, but defeated France in the first World Cup shootout six years later.

In a shootout, five players per side are chosen to take one penalty each, all at one end of the pitch. A shootout is not considered to be part of the actual match, meaning that a goal is not added to a player's season or career tally. Neither penalty takers nor team-mates are allowed to score from a rebound – each player has just one shot at glory. The keeper knows this and often does his or her best to intimidate a penalty taker. If the scores are level after each team has taken five penalties, the competition goes into sudden death. Teams take one penalty each until one side misses and the other scores. On the rare occasion that all the players on the pitch, including the goalkeeper, have taken a penalty and the scores are level, the cycle begins again in the same order. Does this ever happen? Occasionally and spectacularly. In 2007, England and Holland played in the semi-final of the European Under-21 championships. It took 32 penalties before the Dutch won.

▲ *AC Milan's Giampaolo Pazzini scores on a penalty kick during the Serie A match between AC Milan and Cesena, February 2015.*

▼ *Juventus keeper Gianluigi Buffon shows excellent reactions to save a penalty from AC Milan's Christian Brocchi during an Italian Super Cup match.*

MOST PENALTIES IN A SHOOTOUT

PENS	SHOOTOUT SCORE	COMPETITION
48	KK Palace 17 Civics 16	Namibian Cup, 2005
44	Argentinos Juniors 20 Racing Club 19	Argentinian league, 1988
40	Obernai 15 ASCA Wittelsheim 15	French Cup, 1996
40	Tunbridge Wells 16 Littlehampton Town 15	English FA Cup, 2005

▲ *Oliver Neuville of Germany keeps his nerve to place a penalty past Argentina's Leonardo Franco. Germany won the shootout 4-2 to book a place in the last four of the 2006 World Cup.*

SNAPSHOT

BAGGIO'S PENALTY MISS

'The difference between heaven and hell is one minute,' said Spanish international Josep Guardiola after an epic 4-3 win over Yugoslavia at Euro 2000. For Italy's Roberto Baggio, six years earlier, it took mere seconds. In the final of the 1994 World Cup, Italy and Brazil were locked in a 0-0 stalemate. Extra time ended and a nerve-shredding penalty shootout began. With Italy 3-2 down, Baggio stepped up to take his side's pressure-laden fifth penalty. He decided to drive the ball down the middle, as he knew that Taffarel, the Brazilian keeper, tended to dive to one side.

Taffarel did dive, but Baggio sent the ball sailing high over the bar to hand the World Cup to Brazil. Baggio later wrote, 'It was the worst moment of my career. I still dream about it. If I could erase a moment from my career, it would be that one.' What is often forgotten is that two Italians before Baggio, Daniele Massaro and the highly experienced Franco Baresi, missed their penalties. Even if Baggio had scored, Brazil would have had the chance to win with their fifth spot kick. That said, the photograph of a crushed Baggio remains the iconic image of the 1994 World Cup.

Roberto Baggio hangs his head in disbelief as Brazilian players celebrate victory in the final of the 1994 World Cup.

FOOTBALL LEGENDS

From France's Zinedine Zidane to Argentina's Lionel Messi, football has been lit up by the talents of thousands of highly committed and skilful players, all of whom have enthralled spectators and inspired their teams to great achievements. Packed into this section are profiles of more than 75 of the finest players to have graced the game.

KEY
Country = international side
Caps = international games
Goals = international goals
(to July 2017)

GAO HONG
China, born 1967
Caps: over 100 Goals: 0

An instinctive shot-stopper, Gao Hong began playing football for her factory team before moving to the Guangdong club in southeast China. She became a member of the Chinese national side in 1989 and played in both the 1995 and 1999 World Cups. Gao was in goal for China's two Asian Games successes, in 1994 and 1998, and she also won a silver medal at the 1996 Olympics. At the end of her international career, she appeared in the WUSA league for the New York Power.

GOALKEEPERS

PETER SCHMEICHEL
Denmark, born 1963
Caps: 129 Goals: 1

After playing for Hvidøvre and then Brøndby, Schmeichel became one of the best keepers of the 1990s after Alex Ferguson took him to Manchester United in 1991 for the modest fee of £550,000. The high point of his international career came with winning the 1992 European Championships, while the silverware poured in at club level. The hugely committed Dane redefined one-on-one goalkeeping, standing menacingly tall and large or bravely sprawling at an attacker's feet. After winning a treble (English Premiership, FA Cup and Champions League) with Manchester United in 1999, he moved to Sporting Lisbon and helped the Portuguese side win its first league title in 17 years.

He made a surprise return to the English Premiership in 2001, with Aston Villa and then Manchester City, before injury forced him to retire.

▲ *Peter Schmeichel makes a typically brave save for Manchester City in 2002.*

IKER CASILLAS
Spain, born 1981
Caps: 167 Goals: 0

Spain's number one keeper for more than a decade, Casillas played over 700 times for Real Madrid, with whom he won five La Liga titles, before moving to Porto in 2015. In 2000, he became the youngest goalkeeper to play in a Champions League final, which Real won 3-0. With his razor-sharp reflexes and superb positioning, Casillas has been voted keeper of the year five times and has captained Spain to two European Championship titles and the 2010 World Cup.

▶ *Iker Casillas focuses up the pitch during a 2013 La Liga match between Real Madrid and Valencia.*

FACTFILE Peter Schmeichel showed great striker skills in the 1995-96 UEFA Cup when he came up for an attack and scored with a header against Russian side Rotor Volgograd.

BEST GOALKEEPER AT THE WORLD CUP

Since 1994, FIFA has given an award to the best keeper of the tournament.

YEAR	WINNER
1994	Michel Preud'homme (Belgium)
1998	Fabien Barthez (France)
2002	Oliver Kahn (Germany)
2006	Gianluigi Buffon (Italy)
2010	Iker Casillas (Spain)
2014	Manuel Neuer (Germany)

LEV YASHIN
Soviet Union, 1929-90
Caps: 75 Goals: 0

In South America, Yashin was called the Black Spider. In Europe he was the Black Panther; but everywhere he was regarded as the finest goalkeeper of his era and, possibly, of all time. Blessed with extraordinary anticipation and agility, Yashin made countless, seemingly impossible saves and stopped as many as 150 penalties during his career, which was spent entirely at Moscow Dynamo. In 1954, he made his debut for the national team. Yashin's bravery, vision and shot-stopping skills helped the Soviets to an Olympic title in 1956, the European Championships crown in 1960 and a semi-final place at the 1966 World Cup. With Moscow Dynamo, Yashin won six league titles and two Soviet Cups. In 1963, he became the first – and still the only – goalkeeper to win the coveted European Player of the Year award.

▲ Lev Yashin makes a great save at the 1966 World Cup.

GORDON BANKS
England, born 1937
Caps: 73 Goals: 0

'Banks of England' was as secure a keeper as any nation could call upon in the 1960s. During his ten-year international career, he kept 35 clean sheets and was on the losing side just nine times. His professional career began at Chesterfield, before a £7,000 move took him to Leicester City. In 1962, Banks made his debut for England, with whom he won the 1966 World Cup. The following year, he moved to Stoke City, but a car crash in 1972 caused Banks to lose the sight in his right eye. The accident ended his career in Britain, although he did play in the USA for the Fort Lauderdale Strikers in 1977–78.

FACTFILE
Gordon Banks won FIFA's Goalkeeper of the Year award a record six times.

▲ Gordon Banks in action for Stoke City in 1972. Throughout his career, Banks trained tirelessly on angles and repeat drills to improve his strength and agility.

MATCH ACTION

Brazil and England played a tense yet thrilling match in the group stages of the 1970 World Cup, with Brazil winning 1-0. In the tenth minute, Jairzinho slipped a high cross into the English penalty area. Rising high, Pelé headed the ball down fiercely towards the far post, with Gordon Banks seemingly stranded. The ball bounced just short of the line and a goal seemed certain. Yet Banks showed electrifying reactions, scrambling across his line and clawing the ball almost vertically upwards and over the crossbar. Pelé was stunned and later called it 'the greatest save I ever saw'. Few who witnessed it would disagree.

Tommy Wright

Pelé

Alan Mullery

Banks 2

Banks 1

Tostao

PAT JENNINGS
Northern Ireland, born 1945
Caps: 119 Goals: 0

Calm, gentle and seemingly unflappable, Northern Ireland's Pat Jennings famously received no formal coaching before joining his local team, Newry Town. A short spell with Watford followed, before he moved to Tottenham Hotspur in 1964. There he won the FA Cup, two League Cups and the UEFA Cup. In the 1967 Charity Shield match against Manchester United, a kick from Jennings sailed over the head of the opposing keeper, Alex Stepney, to score a memorable goal. Jennings was sold to Tottenham's north London rivals Arsenal in 1977, where he played for eight seasons. He came out of retirement to play his 119th game for his country at the 1986 World Cup.

▶ Dino Zoff organizes Italy's defence during the 1982 World Cup. Voted Italian goalkeeper of the century, Zoff once remained unbeaten in goal for Juventus for ten games.

DINO ZOFF
Italy, born 1942
Caps: 112 Goals: 0

A true goalkeeping legend, Dino Zoff was rejected as a 14-year-old by both Juventus and Internazionale for being too small. He finally signed for Udinese before moving to Mantova and then Napoli. In 1972, Zoff was bought by Juventus, where he won six Italian league titles, two Italian Cups and a UEFA Cup. Zoff's first international call-up came during the 1968 European Championships. He debuted in the quarter-finals and was part of the side that won the final. A model athlete with intense concentration, Zoff broke many goalkeeping records (see page 23) and in 1982, at the age of 40, he captained Italy to their first World Cup success in the modern era. The oldest player to win a World Cup, Zoff retired shortly afterwards and went on to coach Italy's Olympic team, Juventus and Lazio. He coached Italy to the final of Euro 2000, where they lost narrowly to France.

▲ Manuel Neuer was voted German footballer of the year for the 2014–15 season, a rare accolade for a goalkeeper.

MANUEL NEUER
Germany, born 1986
Caps: 74 Goals: 0

A dynamic sweeper-keeper, comfortable on the ball and brilliant in one-on-one situations, Neuer joined Schalke 04 in 1991 and didn't leave until 2011 when he moved for a record fee of 22 million euros to Bayern Munich. He made an instant impact, notching up over 1,000 minutes without conceding a goal in a string of games in his first season, winning three Bundesliga titles and the 2012–13 Champions League. Debuting internationally in 2009, he only conceded one goal in Germany's Euro 2012 campaign. More was to come in 2014 when he became a World Cup winner and was voted goalkeeper of the tournament.

HOPE SOLO
USA, born 1981
Caps: 202 Goals: 0

The USA number one keeper since 2005, Solo started her professional career with Philadelphia Charge in 2003 before having spells in Sweden and France and returning to the US with a succession of WUSA and WPS teams. In 2013, she joined the Seattle Reign in the newly formed National Women's Soccer League. She has won Olympic gold twice (2008, 2012) and was a member of the USA team that were runners-up at the 2011 World Cup. Solo was voted keeper of the World Cup, a feat she repeated four years later as five clean sheets helped her side become 2015 champions.

▲ Pat Jennings tips the ball over the bar during a World Cup qualifying game against England in 1985.

FACTFILE Between 1966 and 1977, Sepp Maier played an astonishing 422 consecutive games for Bayern Munich.

DEFENDERS

MARCEL DESAILLY
France, born 1968
Caps: 116 Goals: 3

Marcel Desailly is world-famous as one of the French players who won the World Cup and European Championship crowns in 1998 and 2000. He was born in the African nation of Ghana and came to France as a young child. A skilful and commanding central defender, Desailly began his career with FC Nantes and then Olympique Marseille. In 1993, he won the Champions League with Marseille, before moving to AC Milan and winning the Champions League again the following year. After a series of outstanding performances at the 1998 World Cup, Desailly moved to Chelsea, where he proved a popular leader. In 2004, Desailly retired from international football and left Chelsea to join Qatar's Al-Ittihad club.

▲ Marcel Desailly hits a long pass during France's 1998 World Cup game against Denmark.

FACTFILE World Cup winner Marcel Desailly became the third player to be sent off in a World Cup final when he was dismissed against Brazil in 1998 after receiving two yellow cards.

▲ In 1978, Daniel Passarella captained Argentina to the World Cup trophy on home soil

DANIEL PASSARELLA
Argentina, born 1953
Caps: 70 Goals: 22

Passarella was a gifted central defender who made surging runs into midfield to build attacks. He was exceptionally good in the air despite being of average height, and struck devastating free kicks. In 298 Argentinian league matches, he scored an astonishing 99 goals. Passarella had success with River Plate before a move to Europe in 1982, first to Fiorentina and then to Internazionale. In 1985–86, he scored 11 goals for Fiorentina, a record for a defender that lasted for 15 years. He won the 1978 World Cup, played in the 1982 tournament and was picked for 1986, but was sidelined through injury. After retiring, Passarella became a coach, managing Argentina at the 1998 World Cup.

ELIAS FIGUEROA
Chile, born 1946
Caps: 47 Goals: 2

This elegant and skilled defender played almost all of his football in the left-back position. Figueroa appeared in three World Cups – 1966, 1974 and 1982 – and in 1974 he was voted the best defender of the tournament. He won the South American Footballer of the Year award an unprecedented three times in a row (1974–76). At club level, Figueroa won league titles in three different countries – the Chilean league with Colo Colo twice, the Brazilian league with Internacional on three occasions and the Uruguayan league with Peñarol five times. He ended his career in the USA, playing for the Fort Lauderdale Strikers alongside Gerd Müller and Teofilio Cubillas, the great Peruvian striker.

RUNE BRATSETH
Norway, born 1961
Caps: 60 Goals: 4

Rune Bratseth began his football career with Rosenborg Trondheim, but did not turn professional until the age of 23. In 1986, he moved to Germany's Werder Bremen for just £65,000. Bremen had bought a bargain, as Bratseth became their defensive linchpin, using his great pace and skill to operate as a centre-back or a sweeper. Bratseth won two Bundesliga titles and a European Cup-Winners' Cup with Bremen, and was twice voted Germany's best foreign import. One of his proudest moments came in 1994, when he captained Norway to their first World Cup finals since 1938. After the tournament, he retired and went on to became director of coaching at Rosenborg.

◀ Rune Bratseth powers away from the Republic of Ireland's John Aldridge at the 1994 World Cup.

BOBBY MOORE
England, 1941-93
Caps: 108 Goals: 2

England's finest ever defender, Moore appeared to lack the pace and the commanding physique to be a great central defender. However, he was blessed with a wonderful eye for the game and always appeared to be one step ahead of opposition attackers. His tackling was clean and surgical, and he was very rarely cautioned. One of football's truly outstanding captains, Moore led England in 90 games – a record shared with Billy Wright – including the 1966 World Cup triumph. He spent most of his career at West Ham, only joining Fulham (alongside George Best) at the age of 32, before finally moving to the USA to play for Seattle Sounders and San Antonio Thunder. His friendship with Pelé was cemented in 1970, when the two men played out an epic struggle for supremacy in England's World Cup game against Brazil. Pelé called Moore the greatest defender he had played against.

◄ *Bobby Moore, England's captain, celebrates with the 1966 World Cup.*

▲ *Matthias Sammer (left) was the first defender to win the European Player of the Year award since Franz Beckenbauer in 1976.*

MATTHIAS SAMMER
East Germany / Germany,
born 1967 Caps: 74 Goals: 14

Matthias Sammer followed in the footsteps of his father, who played in midfield for East Germany and Dresden. As a midfielder, Sammer led East Germany to victory at the 1986 European Youth Championships. After Germany reunified in 1990, he moved into defence and was a commanding sweeper in the 1994 World Cup and two European Championships. A move to the Italian club Internazionale was short-lived and he returned to Germany to join Borussia Dortmund, with whom he won two Bundesliga titles and the 1997 Champions League. In 1996, he became the first player from the former East Germany to win the European Footballer of the Year award.

PAOLO MALDINI
Italy, born 1968
Caps: 126 Goals: 7

One of the best defenders in world football, Paolo Maldini was a one-club player. He made his first-team debut for AC Milan in 1985 and played over 900 games for the Italian club, mostly at left-back, although he would also play as a central defender or as a sweeper. Maldini was able to read the game extremely well, tackle cleanly and move the ball forwards accurately. He debuted for Italy in 1988 and soon became a regular in the national side. He played in four World Cups and four European Championships, retiring from international football after the 2002 World Cup. Winning seven Serie A titles, Maldini also lifted the Champions League trophy in 2003 and 2007. He eventually retired just short of his 41st birthday.

◄ *Paolo Maldini, Italy's longest-serving defender, clears the ball out of his penalty area during the 1994 World Cup final against Brazil.*

THIAGO SILVA
Brazil, born 1984
Caps: 61   Goals: 4

Tough and skilful, Silva can play in any position across the defence and actually started out as a midfielder in Brazil but moved to Europe in 2004. After spells at Porto and Dynamo Moscow, where he contracted tuberculosis and nearly quit football, Silva joined Fluminense and helped them to win their first ever Copa do Brazil in 2007. AC Milan paid around 10 million euros to bring him back to Europe in 2009, where he won the 2010–11 Serie A before becoming the world's most expensive defender with a move to Paris Saint-Germain. Silva captained Brazil when they won the 2013 FIFA Confederations Cup and has played at two Olympic Games, winning a bronze medal in 2008 and a silver in 2012.

▲ *Holland's Ruud Krol at the 1980 European Championships, which were held in Italy.*

FACTFILE
Ruud Krol held the record as the most-capped Dutch player for 21 years. His total was finally overtaken in 2000.

▶ *Franz Beckenbauer at the 1974 World Cup. Sixteen years later, he became the second man – after Brazil's Mario Zagalo – to have won the World Cup as both a player and a manager.*

RUUD KROL
Holland, born 1949
Caps: 83
Goals: 4

Krol was a vital part of the great Ajax and Holland 'total football' sides of the late 1960s and 1970s, comfortable playing in almost any defensive position. With Ajax he won six league titles and two European Cups (1972 and 1973). Krol was the last of the Ajax greats to move away, when in 1980 he played for Vancouver Whitecaps in Canada. He returned to Europe the following year to play for Napoli and later for Cannes in the French second division, where injury forced him to retire in 1987. He has since managed in a variety of countries, including Switzerland, Egypt and Belgium.

FRANZ BECKENBAUER
West Germany, born 1945
Caps: 103   Goals: 14

Der Kaiser made his debut for Bayern Munich in 1964 as an attacking inside-left. Just 27 games later, he was in the national side. At the 1966 World Cup, Beckenbauer played in midfield and scored four goals on the way to the final. By the 1970 tournament, he had moved into defence, where he revolutionized the ultra-defensive role of sweeper with his astonishing vision and silky skills on the ball. Time and again he would turn defence into attack, striding up the pitch to release team-mates or take a chance himself. With his stylish attacking play, it is sometimes forgotten that he was a masterful defender, always cool under pressure. In 1972, Beckenbauer won the European Championships with West Germany and was European Footballer of the Year. Two years later, he won the first of three consecutive European Cups with Bayern Munich and also captained his country to World Cup glory. In 1977, he made a surprise move to the USA, playing in a star-studded New York Cosmos team before returning to Germany in 1980 with Hamburg. He became West Germany's coach in 1984, leading the team to two World Cup finals and winning one.

HIT THE NET

www.planetworldcup.com/LEGENDS/wcstars.html
A selection of profiles of many great footballers, including Austria's Hans Krankl, Belgium's Jan Ceulemans and West Germany's Karl-Heinz Rummenigge.

www.rsssf.com/miscellaneous/century.html
A regularly updated list of footballers with 100 or more international caps. Clicking on a player's name reveals a list of all their international matches.

http://www.theguardian.com/football/series/world-cup-s-top-100-footballers
Profiles of 100 great players from past World Cups.

▲ *Franco Baresi won three European Cups with AC Milan, including this triumph in 1989.*

FRANCO BARESI
Italy, born 1960
Caps: 81 Goals: 1

A tough, intelligent defender, Baresi made his first-team debut for AC Milan in 1978. He played 716 games for the club, winning six Serie A titles. Baresi had to wait until 1990 to break fully into the Italian national team, however. Although part of the 1982 World Cup squad, he was not picked to play and refused to appear for Italy while Enzo Bearzot remained manager. He played in both the 1990 and 1994 World Cups and superbly cancelled out the threat of Brazil's Romario and Bebeto in the 1994 final, which Italy lost only on penalties. Milan paid him the ultimate tribute on his retirement in 1997, dropping the number six shirt from their line-up.

HONG MYUNG-BO
South Korea, born 1969
Caps: 136 Goals: 10

An excellent passer of the ball, Hong played for Pohang Steelers in South Korea and for Bellmare Hiratsuke (now Shonan Bellmare) and Kashiwa Reysol in Japan. He is South Korea's most-capped player and a veteran of four World Cups. At the 2002 tournament, where South Korea reached the semi-finals on home soil, Hong was voted the third best player of the World Cup behind Oliver Kahn and Ronaldo. In November 2002, he became the first Korean to play in the American MLS when he signed for Los Angeles Galaxy.

LINDA MEDALEN
Norway, born 1965
Caps: 152 Goals: 64

Medalen started her career as a striker, making her debut for Norway in 1987 and going on to win the 1988 unofficial Women's World Cup and the 1993 European Championships. At the 1991 World Cup she was her side's top scorer, with six goals, as Norway finished runners-up. As Medalen's career progressed, she moved into defence, where her skill in the air and strong tackling helped Norway to win the 1995 World Cup, conceding just one goal in six games. Medalen played in the 1999 tournament, but a knee injury kept her out of the 2000 Olympics, which Norway won. At club level, she won five league championships and three cup competitions for the Norwegian side Asker SKK.

◄ *Linda Medalen holds off China's Ying Liu in the 1999 World Cup semi-final. The Norwegian retired a year later.*

JOHN CHARLES
Wales, 1931–2004
Caps: 38 Goals: 21

The gloriously talented Charles was equally skilled as a bustling, powerful centre-forward or as a hugely commanding central defender. In both positions, he was world class. Appearing in attack for Leeds United, he scored a record 42 goals in one season, while playing internationally as a central defender. In the Welsh side, Charles was joined by his brother, Mel, and team-mates Ivor and Len Allchurch – the first time that any national side had included two pairs of brothers. In 1957, the British transfer record was smashed as he moved to Juventus for £67,000. Charles became a genuine legend in Italy for his towering performances, generous behaviour towards fans and his sportsmanship. In a highly defence-minded league, he scored an astonishing 93 goals in 155 matches, helping Juve win three Serie A titles and two Italian Cups. He later moved back to Leeds, then on to Parma, Cardiff City and Hereford United, before retiring.

◄ *John Charles (right) battles for the ball at the 1958 World Cup. Charles' name is still revered by Juventus fans, who nicknamed him Il Buon Gigante – the Gentle Giant.*

MIDFIELDERS AND WINGERS

LANDON DONOVAN
USA, born 1982
Caps: 157 Goals: 57

Donovan came to prominence early when he was voted the best player of the 1999 FIFA Under-17 World Championship and was signed the same year by Bayer Leverkusen. Returning to the USA on loan with the San Jose Earthquakes, Donovan would later have short loan spells with Bayern Munich and Everton, but in 2005 he joined the LA Galaxy.

He has won five MLS Cups, three with LA Galaxy and two with the San Jose Earthquakes, as well as winning the CONCACAF Gold Cup three times with the US team. Two-footed and capable of devastating attacking bursts from midfield, Donovan's eye for a goal has seen him score more than 150 times in the MLS and other US club competitions. His 57 goals make him, far and away, the US national team's most prolific goal scorer.

◄ *Landon Donovan goes to turn with the ball during an MLS game between LA Galaxy and the Portland Timbers.*

STANLEY MATTHEWS
England, 1915-2000
Caps: 54 Goals: 11

The 'Wizard of the Dribble' made his first-team debut for Stoke City in 1932 and went on to amaze crowds with his sensational wing play, supreme control and ability to dribble through a defence at will. Matthews' dedication to fitness, years ahead of his time, ensured that his career was one of the longest in British football. He joined Blackpool in 1947 and inspired them to an incredible FA Cup triumph in 1953, in what is remembered as the 'Matthews final'. His England career ran from 1937 to 1954, although he only played in 54 of the 119 internationals the team contested, to the outrage of his many fans. He became the first winner of the European Footballer of the Year award in 1956, and in 1961 he returned to Stoke, for whom he played his last game in 1965, aged 50 years and five days. In the same year, he became the first ever serving footballer to be knighted.

▲ *Stanley Matthews (left) exhibits supreme poise, balance and skill on the ball as he takes on Scotland's George Young in 1948.*

FACTFILE Stanley Matthews was praised as one of the most modest and sporting players to ever grace the game. In his 33-year-long career, he never received a booking.

CARLOS VALDERRAMA
Colombia, born 1961
Caps: 110 Goals: 10

Famous for his flamboyant play and hairstyle, Carlos Valderrama was an exquisite passer of the ball in midfield, who would often link with the attack to devastating effect. He played for three Colombian teams – Union Magdalena, Millionarios and Deportiva Cali – before moving to France in 1988, where he won the league title with Montpellier. In 1996, he moved to the USA to play for Tampa Bay Mutiny and then Miami Fusion. Valderrama captained Colombia to three World Cup tournaments in a row (1990–98) and retired from international football after the 1998 tournament. Yet, even past his 40th birthday, Valderrama was still one of the biggest stars in the MLS.

► *Carlos Valderrama on the ball during Colombia's 1998 World Cup game against England.*

ALAIN GIRESSE
France, born 1952
Caps: 47 Goals: 6

At 1.63m tall and weighing around 60kg, Giresse was small for competitive football, but his tireless work in midfield caught the eye both at club level, for Bordeaux and Olympique Marseille, and with the French national team. Giresse appeared at two World Cups (1982 and 1986) and also won the 1984 European Championships. He played more than 500 matches for Bordeaux and scored the winning goal in the 1986 French Cup final against Marseille, whom he joined a few weeks later. Giresse went on to manage Paris Saint-Germain and Toulouse. After coaching for the national teams of Georgia, Gabon and Mali, in 2013 he took over as head coach for Senegal.

HRISTO STOICHKOV
Bulgaria, born 1966
Caps: 83 Goals: 37

As an attacking midfielder or a striker, the strong, stocky Stoichkov was surprisingly quick over a short distance and possessed unstoppable power, particularly in his left foot. He emerged as a skilful youngster at CSKA Sofia before moving to Barcelona. Unpredictable and prone to tempers, Stoichkov fell out with Barcelona manager Johan Cruyff when he was asked to play out wide. He later moved to Parma, Japanese side Kashiwa Reysol and the Chicago Fire in the MLS. He arrived at the 1994 World Cup as the star player in an underrated Bulgarian side that sensationally knocked out Germany before losing the semi-final to Italy. Stoichkov finished the tournament as joint top scorer. It was his finest hour as a player.

FACTFILE Stoichkov was banned for the 1985-86 season for his part in a riot involving players and supporters at the 1985 Bulgarian Cup final.

▲ *Stoichkov during the Euro '96 match against Romania. The midfielder's goal won the game.*

DAVID BECKHAM
England, born 1975
Caps: 115 Goals: 17

David Beckham is one of the most recognizable footballers on the planet. He began his career as a youth-team player at Manchester United, then had a loan spell with Preston North End, before announcing his arrival in English football with a Premiership goal from inside his own half against Wimbledon. At the 1998 World Cup he was heavily criticized for kicking out at Argentina's Diego Simeone and receiving a red card. But Beckham's excellence for club and country, particularly his trademark swerving free kicks, won back public support – notably when he ensured England's qualification for the 2002 World Cup with a last-gasp goal against Greece. He also won 'the treble' of Champions League, Premiership and FA Cup with Manchester United in 1999. When David Beckham joined Paris Saint-Germain, in 2013, he donated his entire salary to a local children's charity. He became the first English player to win the league in four different countries (England, Spain, the USA and France).

▶ *In 2006, David Beckham became the first English player to score in three World Cups. He resigned as captain straight after the tournament.*

ANDRÉS INIESTA
Spain, born 1984
Caps: 116 Goals: 12

Quick feet and an even quicker footballing brain has enabled this slight midfielder to become one of the most celebrated players in world football. Joining Barcelona as a youth teamer, Iniesta later formed a formidable central midfield partnership with Xavi Hernández for both club and country. With Barcelona, he has won seven Spanish league championships, four Champions Leagues and five Spanish Super Cups. Internationally, he has been a crucial part of Spain's success, and scored the winning goal in the 2010 World Cup final.

▲ *Spanish midfield legend Xavi Hernández.*

XAVI HERNÁNDEZ
Spain, born 1980
Caps: 133 Goals: 12

Rising through the ranks of youth and reserve teams at Barcelona, Xavi made his first team debut in 1998 and played over 750 games for the Spanish club before moving to Qatar in 2015 to play for Al Sadd. With Barcelona, he won eight La Liga titles and four Champions Leagues and enjoyed Euro 2008 and 2012 and 2010 World Cup glory with Spain. Brilliant at finding space even in the most crowded parts of the pitch, Xavi is a passing maestro – enabling his side to keep possession and attack.

MICHEL PLATINI
France, born 1955
Caps: 72   Goals: 41

A truly great attacking midfielder, Platini was the glittering jewel in a French side that suffered semi-final heartbreak at the 1982 World Cup. Two years later, he was top scorer at the European Championships (nine goals) as France won the title. In partnership with Alan Giresse and Jean Tigana, Platini exhibited immense skill and vision. At club level, Platini played for AS Joeuf, Nancy and Saint-Étienne before turning down a transfer to Arsenal in favour of Italian giants Juventus in 1982. He was Serie A's leading marksman three times and was crowned European Footballer of the Year three times in a row (1983–85) – a unique achievement. Retiring in 1987, he went on to manage France and then led his country's bid to host the 1998 World Cup. In 2007, he became president of UEFA.

▲ *Platini skips a challenge during France's 4-1 win over Northern Ireland at the 1982 World Cup.*

▲ *Dragan Dzajic (left) and Willie Morgan wave to the crowd after Yugoslavia's 1-1 draw with Scotland at the 1974 World Cup.*

FACTFILE Garrincha retired in 1966, after Brazil's loss to Hungary in the World Cup. Astonishingly, in his 50 matches it was the only time he was on the losing side for Brazil.

GARRINCHA
Brazil, 1933–83
Caps: 50
Goals: 12

Manuel Francisco dos Santos was nicknamed Garrincha – meaning 'little bird' – at a young age. A small player at only 1.69m tall, a childhood illness had left his legs distorted, with one bent inwards and the other 6cm shorter. Yet those who saw Garrincha play remember him as the greatest dribbler in the history of football. He also perfected the bending banana kick, which he used to great effect for his club side, Botafogo, scoring 232 goals in 581 matches. He also played in Colombia, Italy, and in France for Red Star Paris, but it was on the international stage that Garrincha became famous. He starred in the 1958

DRAGAN DZAJIC
Yugoslavia, born 1946
Caps: 85   Goals: 23

A left-winger for his entire career, Dragan Dzajic boasted lightning-fast acceleration and an eye for a delicate pass. He made over 580 appearances for Red Star Belgrade, scoring 287 goals, winning five Yugoslav league titles and four Yugoslav Cups. Dzajic also spent two seasons in France, where he scored 31 goals for Bastia. He was part of the Yugoslav side that entered the 1964 Olympics and reached the final of the 1968 European Championships, knocking out World Cup holders England along the way. Dzajic finished the tournament as top scorer. After retiring from football in 1979, he went on to become sports director of Red Star.

▼ *England defender Ray Wilson fails to stop the mesmeric Garrincha as he surges down the wing in the 1962 World Cup quarter-final. Brazil won 3-1.*

World Cup, which Brazil won, but went on to eclipse those performances at the 1962 competition. Voted player of the tournament, he was joint leading scorer as he struck two goals to knock out England in the quarter-final, and then two more to beat Chile in the semi-final. Sadly, his life away from football was troubled, and he died of alcohol poisoning at the age of 49.

CRISTIANO RONALDO
Portugal, born 1985
Caps: 138 Goals: 71

A winger who can play in central midfield or as a striker, Cristiano Ronaldo began playing football on the Portuguese island of Madeira before joining Sporting Clube de Portugal. After impressing Sir Alex Ferguson in a pre-season friendly, Ronaldo joined Manchester United in 2003, where he blossomed into one of the world's greatest attackers, bewildering defenders with tricks and pace, outstanding ball control and masterful free kicks. His club performances helped to propel Manchester United to three successive Premier League titles as well as the Champions League crown in 2008, the same year that he won FIFA's World Footballer of the Year. Ronaldo left United in July 2009, joining Real Madrid for a world-record fee of £80 million. He made a huge impact, notching a staggering 390 goals in his first 382 games to become the club's all-time leading scorer, as well as captaining Portugal to Euro 2016 glory in the same year he won his fourth FIFA world's best player award.

FACTFILE Cristiano Ronaldo has scored 50 or more goals a season for five seasons in a row and has scored a record 32 hat-tricks for Real Madrid.

▲ Portugal's Cristiano Ronaldo races forwards with the ball at his feet. After Euro 2008, he was appointed captain of the national side.

ZINEDINE ZIDANE
France, born 1972
Caps: 108 Goals: 31

The son of Algerian immigrants, Zidane grew up in Marseille with posters of his idol, Enzo Francescoli of Uruguay, on his wall. His first club was Cannes, followed by Bordeaux, where he won France's Young Player of the Year award in 1992. In his international debut in 1994, he scored both of France's goals in a 2-2 draw with the Czech Republic. In 1995–96, Zidane played 57 matches – more than any other French player – and he appeared jaded as he underperformed at Euro '96. But a move to Juventus in the same year saw him regain his best form, as he helped the Serie A giants win two league titles. Zidane was a key part of the French side that captured a double of World Cup (1998) and European Championships (2000). As the best midfielder in the world, he won World Player of the Year titles in 1998, 2000 and 2003. Zidane's last tournament, the 2006 World Cup, was memorable as he led France to the final, scoring three goals on the way and being voted FIFA's player of the tournament. He was sent off in the final, however, for a headbutt to the chest of Italy's Marco Materazzi.

ENZO SCIFO
Belgium, born 1966
Caps: 84 Goals: 18

One of only a handful of players to have taken part in four World Cups, Vicenzo 'Enzo' Scifo (see page 87) was born to Italian parents and became a Belgian citizen at the age of 18. He was a footballing prodigy, scoring a staggering 432 goals in just four seasons as a junior. After joining Anderlecht in 1980, his silky midfield skills helped the club to three Belgian league titles in a row (1985–87), while with the national side he reached the semi-finals of the 1986 World Cup. Scifo's moves to Internazionale and then Bordeaux were both failures, but his career was reignited at Auxerre. He went on to enjoy spells in Italy, before rejoining Anderlecht towards the end of his career.

WORLD-RECORD TRANSFERS

PLAYER	FROM	TO	FEE	YEAR
Paul Pogba (France)	Juventus	Manchester United	£89.3m	2016
Gareth Bale (Wales)	Tottenham	Real Madrid	£85.3m	2013
Cristiano Ronaldo (Portugal)	Manchester Utd	Real Madrid	£80m	2009
Gonzalo Higuain (Argentina)	Napoli	Juventus	£75.3m	2016
Luis Suarez (Uruguay)	Liverpool	Barcelona	£65m	2014
James Rodriguez (Colombia)	AS Monaco	Real Madrid	£63m	2014
Oscar (Brazil)	Chelsea	Shanghai SIPG	£60m	2017
Angel di Maria (Argentina)	Real Madrid	Manchester United	£59.7m	2014
Zlatan Ibrahimovic (Sweden)	Internazionale	Barcelona	£56.9m	2009
Kaka (Brazil)	AC Milan	Real Madrid	£56.1m	2009
Edinson Cavani (Uruguay)	Napoli	Paris Saint-Germain	£55.6m	2013

LUIS FIGO
Portugal, born 1972
Caps: 127 Goals: 32

A darting wide midfielder, Luis Figo won the European Cup-Winners' Cup in 1997 and back-to-back Spanish league titles in 1998 and 1999 with Spanish giants Barcelona. He moved for a world-record fee to Barcelona's fiercest rivals, Real Madrid, winning two league titles and the Champions League in 2002. Figo played at three European Championships, reaching the semi-finals in 2000 and the final four years later. In 2005, he came out of international retirement to help Portugal qualify for the 2006 World Cup, where they reached the semi-final.

▲ *Hagi pushes forwards at the 1994 World Cup.*

GHEORGHE HAGI
Romania, born 1965
Caps: 125 Goals: 34

Moody, unpredictable and outstandingly skilful, Hagi played for Steaua Bucharest from 1987, either in midfield or in a free role in attack. His superb ball skills and vision helped his club to three league titles in a row, as well as to the 1989 European Cup final. Hagi then played for Real Madrid, Brescia, Barcelona and Galatasaray, with whom he won the 2000 UEFA Cup. A linchpin of the Romanian team, Hagi scored a sublime goal from 35 metres out against Colombia at the 1994 World Cup, but he was sent off in his final international match, at Euro 2000.

▲ *Boniek scored all three goals in this 3-0 victory for Poland over Belgium at the 1982 World Cup.*

ZBIGNIEW BONIEK
Poland, born 1956
Caps: 80 Goals: 24

A hard-running attacking midfielder, Boniek won two league titles with Widzew Lodz and starred when the Polish side knocked Juventus out of the 1980 UEFA Cup. He joined the Italian club two years later and formed a deadly midfield partnership with Michel Platini. At Juventus, he won Italian league and cup titles, the European Cup-Winners' Cup and the 1985 European Cup (scoring the two winning goals). A member of three World Cup squads, Boniek scored four goals in 1982 as Poland came third. After joining Roma in 1985, he operated deeper and deeper in midfield and he played as a sweeper in the 1986 World Cup.

> **FACTFILE** Michael Laudrup is the only player to have appeared for Real Madrid in a 5-0 win over Barcelona and also for Barcelona when they have beaten Real 5-0.

SOCRATES
Brazil, 1954–2014
Caps: 60 Goals: 22

Named after the Ancient Greek scholar, Brazil's Socrates played as an amateur for Botafogo while studying to become a doctor. He turned professional with Corinthians in 1977. The tall, elegant midfielder became a firm favourite with the fans, scoring spectacular goals and threading superb passes around the pitch. He captained two hugely talented Brazilian World Cup sides in 1982 and 1986, but neither team did its talent justice.

> **FACTFILE**
> In November 2004, at the age of 50, Socrates played for English non-league side Garforth Town in the Northern Counties League.

MICHAEL LAUDRUP
Denmark, born 1964
Caps: 104 Goals: 37

The peak of Michael Laudrup's international career came in the quarter-finals of the 1998 World Cup, where Denmark lost narrowly to Brazil 3-2 – despite his younger brother, Brian, scoring a goal. Laudrup was much in demand as an attacking midfielder, playing for Lazio and Juventus in Italy and winning five league titles in Spain with Barcelona and Real Madrid. Sadly, he missed out on Denmark's finest hour – their Euro '92 championship triumph, when he argued about tactics with the coach and was dropped.

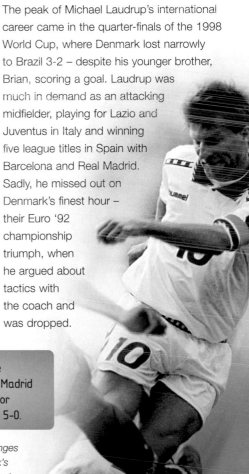

▶ *Michael Laudrup challenges for the ball during Denmark's Euro '96 match with Portugal.*

▲ *Lothar Matthäus appeared at five World Cups.*

LOTHAR MATTHÄUS
West Germany / Germany,
born 1961 Caps: 150 Goals: 23

Matthäus began his career at Borussia Mönchengladbach before moving to Bayern Munich in 1984. A powerful midfielder with great stamina, Matthäus could play as a midfield anchor or be more creative, using his passing and vision to bring others into the game. He won six Bundesliga titles at Bayern Munich, plus the Serie A title with Internazionale. A veteran of five World Cups, Matthäus played a record 25 tournament games. He led West Germany to World Cup glory in 1990 and in the same year he was voted World Footballer of the Year. He retired from international football after Euro 2000.

MARIO COLUNA
Portugal, 1935–2014
Caps: 57 Goals: 8

Like Eusebio, Mario Coluna was born in Mozambique and played for Portugal. Coluna was often overshadowed by the great striker, but he was a superb footballer in his own right. His 17-year career with Benfica began in 1954. He captained the side in the early 1960s and appeared in five European Cup finals (1961–63, 1965 and 1968). He also led Portugal to third place in the 1966 World Cup. Coluna moved to Olympique Lyonnais towards the end of his career and later became Mozambique's minister of sport.

SUN WEN
China, born 1973
Caps: 152 Goals: 106

A legend in women's football, Sun Wen won seven regional championships with Chinese side Shanghai TV, before moving to the USA in 2000 to play for Atlanta Beat. Playing in midfield or attack, she has become one of the world's leading international goalscorers, thanks to her strong shooting, vision and eye for a goal. Sun Wen won both the Golden Boot (top scorer) and the Golden Ball (top player) awards at the 1999 Women's World Cup, where China were narrowly beaten on penalties in the final by the USA. In 2000, she was named FIFA World Player of the Century alongside the USA's Michelle Akers. After China's surprise World Cup exit at the hands of Canada in 2003, she retired.

▲ *Sun Wen goes past Ghana's Mavis Danso at the 2003 World Cup. China won the game 1-0, courtesy of a goal from Sun.*

JAIRZINHO
Brazil, born 1944
Caps: 82 Goals: 34

Jair Ventura Filho, better known as Jairzinho, was an electrifying right-winger in a similar mould to his childhood hero, Garrincha. First capped for Brazil in 1964, he was moved to the left wing to accommodate Garrincha in the 1966 World Cup. At the 1970 tournament Jairzinho was moved back to his favoured right side, where he shone, scoring in each of the six rounds of the competition – a record to this day. At club level, Jairzinho spent most of his career at Brazil's Botafogo, also having short spells with Marseille in France, Portuguesa in Venezuela and the Brazilian side Cruzeiro, with whom he won the Copa America in 1976.

◀ *Jairzinho surges forwards during the third-place play-off at the 1974 World Cup. Brazil were defeated 1-0 by Poland.*

STRIKERS

JOHAN CRUYFF
Holland, 1947-2016
Caps: 48 Goals: 33

Cruyff was one of the game's finest ever players and a pivotal part of the Dutch 'total football' revolution. Blessed with great vision and remarkable ball skills, he is the only player to have a move named after him – the Cruyff turn. He won three European Cups in a row at Ajax, before following his old boss, Rinus Michels, to Barcelona in 1973 and helping them to win Spanish league and cup titles. Cruyff played as a centre forward, but would drift around the pitch, creating confusion among defenders. His total of 33 goals for Holland would have been higher were it not for his refusal to play in the 1978 World Cup (see page 112). Cruyff later managed both Ajax and Barcelona to success in Europe.

▶ *Johan Cruyff was European Footballer of the Year three times.*

PAOLO ROSSI
Italy, born 1956
Caps: 48 Goals: 20

As a teenager, Paolo Rossi was released by Juventus due to a knee injury, but he went on to star for Italy at the 1978 World Cup. Juve tried to buy him back from Vicenza, but were outbid by Perugia, who paid a world-record fee of £3.5 million. A two-year ban for alleged match-fixing ended just before the 1982 World Cup, by which time Rossi was back at Juventus. After failing to score in the first four games of the tournament, the pressure was mounting. He responded with a fine hat-trick against Brazil, followed by two goals in the semi-final and one in the final to emerge as a World Cup winner and the tournament's leading scorer. Sadly, he was overcome by injuries and he retired in 1987, aged 30.

▼ *Puskas (left) fires in a shot in the 1954 World Cup final against West Germany. His goalscoring ratio at international level – almost one goal per game – was extraordinary.*

FACTFILE In his distinguished career, Puskas won five Spanish league titles, four Hungarian league titles, an Olympic gold medal (1952) and three European Cups.

FERENC PUSKAS
Hungary, 1927-2006
Caps: 84 (4 for Spain)
Goals: 83

A star for his club, Kispest (which became Honved), and his country, Puskas was short, stocky and an average header of the ball. But his sublime skills, vision and thunderbolt of a left-foot shot made him a devastating striker. After the Hungarian revolution in 1956, Puskas searched for a club in western Europe for more than a year. In his thirties and overweight, he was eventually signed by Real Madrid in 1958. He repaid Real's faith by heading the Spanish goalscoring table four times, netting four goals in the 1960 European Cup final and a hat-trick in the 1962 final. In 1966, he began a coaching career, which saw him take Greek side Panathinaikos to the 1971 European Cup final. In 1993, an emotional Puskas was welcomed home to act as caretaker manager of the national team.

FACTFILE George Best made 466 appearances for Manchester United between 1963 and 1974, scoring 178 goals. He was a substitute only once.

GEORGE BEST
Northern Ireland, 1946-2005
Caps: 37 Goals: 9

Best was just 17 when he made his first-team debut for Manchester United. He was the most gifted player to emerge from the British Isles, and its first superstar. A free spirit both on and off the pitch, Best's goalscoring exploits and his eye for an outrageous pass or move quickly made him a legend. He was also a fearless tackler and great dribbler, and was Manchester United's leading scorer five seasons in a row. Sadly, he was denied the biggest stage of all as Northern Ireland failed to qualify for the World Cup during his playing career. In 1974, Best sensationally retired from the game. He made a series of comebacks in England, the USA and, finally, Australia, where he appeared for the Brisbane Lions in 1983.

◀ *George Best was first capped for his country, Northern Ireland, at the tender age of 17.*

LIONEL MESSI
Argentina, born 1987
Caps: 117   Goals: 58

Locals in the Argentinean city of Rosario knew they were seeing a special talent when Messi, not yet in his teens, powered his local children's football team to lose just one game in four years. Moving from Argentina to Spain at the age of 13, Messi was schooled in Barcelona's youth sides before making his official debut for the first team at the age of 17. He has already won seven Spanish league and four UEFA Champions League titles with Barcelona, as well as nine Spanish cup competitions and a 2008 Olympic gold medal with Argentina. His close control, vision and flair is almost unparalleled in the modern game. The 2009–10 season saw Messi score 47 goals, including all four goals in Barcelona's Champions League mauling of Arsenal, and the following season he upped this to a staggering 73 goals in all competitions. Messi has not let up since and in November 2016 scored his 500th goal for Barcelona and is La Liga's all-time leading goalscorer.

▶ *Lionel Messi controls the ball during the 2012–13 season, in which he scored 60 goals.*

DENNIS BERGKAMP
Holland, born 1969
Caps: 79   Goals: 37

Named after the Scottish striker Denis Law, Bergkamp was a product of the famous Ajax youth academy. He played in the Dutch league for the first time in 1986. The most technically gifted Dutch footballer since Johan Cruyff, Bergkamp often played in the space between midfield and attack, where he used his eye for an unexpected pass, plus world-class technique, to create as many goals as he scored. After an unsuccessful spell at Internazionale, Bergkamp moved to Arsenal for £7.5 million in 1995. In his 11 years at the club, he won three Premier League titles and scored or set up more than 280 goals. He retired in May 2006 after the final of the Champions League against Barcelona.

▲ *Dennis Bergkamp brings the ball down moments before his sublime goal against Argentina at the 1998 World Cup.*

FACTFILE Dennis Bergkamp's fear of flying caused the striker to miss many international matches and European games for Arsenal.

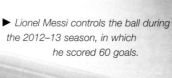

Roa

Ayala 2

Bergkamp 1

Bergkamp 2

Ayala 1

MATCH ACTION

Dennis Bergkamp broke the deadlock in a tense 1998 World Cup quarter-final against Argentina with a sensational goal. On the stroke of 90 minutes, Frank de Boer hit a 50-metre pass into the penalty area. Controlling the ball with one delicate touch of his right boot, Bergkamp took a second touch to turn Argentinian defender Roberto Ayala, before shooting powerfully past keeper Carlos Roa. The goal saw Bergkamp become Holland's leading international scorer.

JUST FONTAINE
France, born 1933
Caps: 21 Goals: 30

Fontaine was born and brought up in Morocco before coming to France in 1953 to play for Nice. A relatively slight centre-forward with a real eye for goal, he scored 45 times in three seasons at Nice before moving to Stade de Reims, where he bagged 116 goals in just four years. Yet, going into the 1958 World Cup finals, Fontaine was third-choice striker behind Raymond Kopa and René Bliard. An injury to Bliard allowed Fontaine to start the first game, against Paraguay, in which he scored a hat-trick. He followed this up with a further ten goals in five games. His record of 13 goals at a single World Cup is unlikely to be beaten. In 1962, Fontaine retired after suffering the second double fracture of his right leg. The following year, he became the first president of the French footballers' union.

ROBERTO BAGGIO
Italy, born 1967
Caps: 57 Goals: 27

Blessed with great skill and vision, Roberto Baggio made his professional debut with Vicenza, in the Italian third division, at just 15 years of age. He broke into Italy's Serie A with Fiorentina in 1985, and when Baggio was transferred to Juventus in 1990, three days of rioting by Fiorentina fans ensued. The fee of £7.7 million made him the world's most expensive player at that time. Crowned World Footballer of the Year in 1993, Baggio scored spectacular goals for his country and his clubs, AC Milan, Bologna, Inter Milan and Brescia. In 2004, while playing for Brescia, he scored his 200th Serie A goal. He appeared in three World Cups and scored five out of Italy's eight goals in the 1994 competition. However, Baggio will always be remembered for his costly penalty miss in the final of the tournament (see page 32). The striker was given an emotional send-off in 2004 when he played for Italy for the first time in five years, in a friendly against Spain.

RAÚL
Spain, born 1977
Caps: 102 Goals: 44

Raúl González Blanco made his debut for the Real Madrid first team at 17 – their youngest ever player – and went on to score six times in his first 11 games. In the years that followed, Raúl became the biggest star in Spanish football and the country's all-time leading goalscorer. At club level, he has won two Spanish league championships and three Champions League titles with Real Madrid. Top scorer in the Spanish league twice, Raúl's goals in the 2003–04 Champions League campaign saw him become the first player to net more than 40 times in the competition.

GERD MÜLLER
West Germany, born 1945
Caps: 62 Goals: 68

The Bomber, as Gerd Müller was nicknamed, holds a series of goalscoring records. From 1963, he scored a club record 365 goals in 427 league matches for Bayern Munich. During 16 years with Bayern, he won four Bundesliga titles, four German Cups and three European Cups. For his country, Müller held one of the greatest international striking records, scoring more than a goal every game. His two strikes against the Soviet Union helped West Germany win the 1972 European Championships. Müller's tally of 14 World Cup goals remained a record until 2006, while his final international goal won West Germany the 1974 World Cup on home soil.

▲ Spain's Raúl was the top scorer during the qualifying rounds for Euro 2000, with ten goals from eight games. Here, he chases down the ball during Euro 2004.

▼ Gerd Müller shoots during West Germany's win over Morocco in the 1970 World Cup.

ZICO
Brazil, born 1953
Caps: 72 Goals: 52

The youngest and smallest of three football-mad brothers, Artur Antunes Coimbra (known as Zico) was given a special diet and training regime to build him up when he first arrived at the Brazilian club Flamengo. Sharp, quick-witted and with the ability to hit an explosive shot or take a deadly, curling free kick, Zico won four Brazilian league titles with Flamengo, as well as the Copa Libertadores and the World Club Cup (both in 1981). He scored a staggering 591 goals in his first 11 seasons with Flamengo and returned to the club in 1985 after a spell at the Italian Serie A side Udinese. Zico retired from international football after the 1986 World Cup finals, but went on to play in Japan for Kashima Antlers. In 2002, he became manager of the Japanese national team.

BOBBY CHARLTON
England, born 1937
Caps: 106   Goals: 49

Apart from a final season with Preston North End, Charlton was a one-club player with Manchester United, for whom he made his debut in 1956. Known around the globe for his trophy-winning exploits in both the World Cup and the European Cup, Charlton was one of the few survivors of the devastating Munich air crash, which claimed the lives of many of his Manchester United team-mates. As a player he showed great sportsmanship and dedication – in training, he even wore a slipper on his right foot to encourage him to pass and shoot with his weaker left foot. Operating as a deep-lying centre-forward with a phenomenal shot from either foot, Charlton remains the record goalscorer for both England and Manchester United, scoring 245 times and making 751 appearances in total for the club. He was knighted in 1994.

▼ Bobby Charlton's 1970 World Cup campaign was his fourth in a row as part of the England squad.

◄ Roger Milla challenges for the ball during Cameroon's second-round victory over Colombia at the 1990 World Cup.

ROGER MILLA
Cameroon, born c.1952
Caps: 81   Goals: 42

Roger Milla's celebratory corner-flag dance remains the most memorable image of the 1990 World Cup, as his four goals helped Cameroon to become the first African side to reach the quarter-finals. In the same year, the veteran striker was voted the African Footballer of the Year. He had won the award before, way back in 1976, the year he moved from Cameroon's Tonnerre Yaoundé to play for Valenciennes in France. Milla went on to play for Monaco, Bastia and Saint-Etienne, and won the African Nations Cup twice with Cameroon (1984 and 1988). At the age of 42, he came out of retirement for the 1994 World Cup to become the oldest ever player and scorer in the competition.

ANDRIY SHEVCHENKO
Ukraine, born 1976
Caps: 111   Goals: 48

Shevchenko scored just one goal in 16 games in his first season at Dynamo Kiev, but his perfect blend of pace and power propelled Kiev to five Ukrainian league titles and strong showings in the Champions League. A multi-million-pound transfer to AC Milan followed in 1999. On three occasions Shevchenko scored 24 goals per season in the ultra-tough Italian league. In 2004, Shevchenko was voted European Footballer of the Year. Two years later he moved to Chelsea for more than £30 million, but returned to Milan on loan for the 2008–09 season. He then returned to Kiev, where he made more than 80 appearances before retiring in 2012.

FACTFILE In 1990, Andriy Shevchenko played for the Kiev under-14 team in a youth tournament in Wales. Welsh striker Ian Rush was so impressed, he gave the young Ukrainian his football boots.

▲ Andriy Shevchenko shoots for Ukraine against England during a friendly international in 2000.

CAROLINA MORACE
Italy, born 1964
Caps: 153   Goals: 105

Italy's finest female player, Morace made her international and Women's Serie A debut at the age of just 14. She went on to win 12 league titles with eight different clubs, and scored more than 500 goals. A lethal finisher, Morace was twice a runner-up with Italy in the European Championships. After retiring in 1999, she became the first female coach of an Italian men's professional team, Viterbese in Serie C. She later became coach of the Italian women's national side.

▲ *Ruud Gullit shoots against England at Euro '88.*

RUUD GULLIT
Holland, born 1962
Caps: 66 Goals: 17

In 1978, the dreadlocked Gullit started out as a sweeper for Dutch side Haarlem. He possessed great attacking flair, stamina, a tough tackle and a sweet pass. He was the subject of feverish transfer activity, moving to Feyenoord, PSV Eindhoven and AC Milan, with whom he won European Cups in 1989 and 1990. After a season at Sampdoria he moved to Chelsea, and in 1996 he was appointed player-manager of the London club. By winning the 1997 FA Cup he became the first non-British manager to lift a major domestic trophy in England.

KENNY DALGLISH
Scotland, born 1951
Caps: 102 Goals: 30

The only player to have scored over 100 goals for both English and Scottish top-division clubs, Dalglish gave defenders nightmares. He became a legend at Celtic – where he won four league titles and four Scottish Cups – thanks to a quicksilver turn and an icy coolness in front of goal. In 1977, Liverpool signed Dalglish as a replacement for Kevin Keegan. He became Liverpool's player-manager in 1985, winning three league titles. He won a fourth in 1995 with Blackburn Rovers to become one of the few managers to win the English league with different clubs.

DIEGO MARADONA
Argentina, born 1960
Caps: 91 Goals: 34

Diego Armando Maradona was a phenomenal footballer. Stocky and with a low centre of gravity, he conjured mesmeric, weaving runs through the tightest defences, lightning turns that left opposition players kicking at thin air and sublime shots, chips and flicks. Maradona debuted aged 15 for Argentinos Juniors. Calls for his inclusion in the 1978 World Cup squad were ignored by Argentina's coach, Cesar Luis Menotti, but he would appear at the next four tournaments. His finest hour came in 1986, when Maradona was the player of the tournament as he skippered an unremarkable side to World Cup victory (see pages 56–57). Maradona captained Argentina at the 1990 World Cup, where he reached the final, but the following year he failed a drugs test and was banned for 15 months. A further failed test during the 1994 World Cup saw him sent home after playing the first two games. His international career was over. Since then Maradona has battled with drug addiction, but in 2000 he was the joint winner of FIFA's Footballer of the Century award with Pelé.

FACTFILE Diego Maradona's moves to Barcelona in 1982 (for £4.2 million) and then to Napoli in 1984 (for £6.9 million) were both world-record transfers. After nine years at Napoli and a spell at Sevilla, he returned to Argentina with Newell's Old Boys and Boca Juniors.

▼ *The magical Maradona brings the ball under control at the 1986 World Cup.*

ALFREDO DI STEFANO
Spain, 1926–2014
Caps: 31 Goals: 23

To many people, di Stefano was the complete player, years ahead of his time. His astonishing energy helped him play all over the pitch – defending, tackling, unselfishly distributing the ball and creating chances for others as well as for himself. Born in a poor suburb of Buenos Aires, he played for his father's old club, River Plate, in a relentless forward line known as *La Máquina* (the Machine). A move to Europe in 1953 saw him become part of the legendary Real Madrid side that dominated Europe in the 1950s and early 1960s. Di Stefano formed a deadly partnership with Ferenc Puskas, scoring in five European Cup finals in a row. Real Madrid player and coach Miguel Muñoz explained: 'The greatness of di Stefano was that with him in your side, you had two players in every position.'

▲ *As well as appearing for Real Madrid (pictured) and Spain, di Stefano also played seven unofficial games for Argentina and four for Colombia.*

JÜRGEN KLINSMANN
West Germany / Germany, born 1964 Caps: 108 Goals: 47

Sharp and athletic around the penalty area and an outstanding goal poacher, Klinsmann was German Footballer of the Year in his first spell at VfB Stuttgart. He then moved to Internazionale, where he won the 1989 Serie A title. He was part of West Germany's 1990 World Cup-winning side, scored five goals in the 1994 competition and captained the team at the 1998 tournament. Klinsmann enjoyed spells with Monaco and, in 1994, the first of two stints with Tottenham Hotspur. The British media and some supporters were suspicious of a player who had a reputation for diving to win free kicks and penalties. But in his first Premiership season, Klinsmann's performances and 29 goals won the support of many fans, and in 1995 he was voted England's Footballer of the Year. The striker moved to Bayern Munich, Sampdoria and Tottenham once more, before retiring in 1998. In 2004, he was appointed Germany's manager and coached an exciting side to third place at the 2006 World Cup.

▲ Jürgen Klinsmann surges forwards with the ball during Germany's Euro '96 qualifying campaign.

FACTFILE Luigi Riva had such a fearsome shot that he once broke the arm of a spectator.

EUSEBIO
Portugal, 1942—2014 Caps: 64 Goals: 41

Eusebio da Silva Ferreira was the first African footballing superstar. Lethal in the air and equipped with a power-packed right-foot shot, he scored an incredible 727 goals in 715 professional games. Eusebio played his early football for Sporting Lourenço Marques in his home country of Mozambique – a Portugese colony at the time. The striker was at the centre of one of the fiercest transfer disputes when he arrived in Portugal. He was virtually kidnapped by Benfica to keep him away from rivals Sporting Lisbon. Benfica's £7,500 purchase proved to be one of the buys of the century. Over a 15-year career with Benfica, Eusebio scored at an awe-inspiring ratio of more than a goal a game. He was the Portuguese league's top goalscorer seven times, twice the leading goalscorer in the whole of Europe and the 1966 World Cup's top scorer, with nine goals for Portugal.

CARLI LLOYD
USA, born 1982 Caps: 235 Goals: 96

A livewire attacker with stamina, pace and a lethal shot, Lloyd played for W-League team New Jersey Splash whilst still at High School. She made her international debut at age 23 and began a fixture in the US women's team that won two Olympic gold medals and the 2015 World Cup. In that competition, Lloyd was at her height, scoring six times, including a hat-trick in the final that featured a goal from the halfway line. Lloyd was made player of the tournament and was also voted the world's best female footballer in both 2015 and 2016. In 2017, after having played for nine American clubs, including Chicago Red Stars and Western New York Flash, she crossed the Atlantic to move to Manchester City.

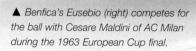

▲ Benfica's Eusebio (right) competes for the ball with Cesare Maldini of AC Milan during the 1963 European Cup final.

GEORGE WEAH
Liberia, born 1966 Caps: 61 Goals: 22

In 1988, the Monaco manager Arsène Wenger (now at Arsenal), shrewdly plucked the young, raw Weah from Cameroon side Tonnerre Yaoundé. Weah exploded onto the European scene, winning the French league with Monaco in 1991 and Paris Saint-Germain in 1994, before moving to AC Milan. A truly devastating finisher, Weah scored many spectacular goals to help AC Milan win two Serie A titles. He was voted African Footballer of the Year four times, and also won European and World Player of the Year awards in 1995 and FIFA's Fair Play Award the following year. He had short spells at Chelsea, Manchester City and in the United Arab Emirates late in his career, before retiring in 2002. A UNICEF ambassador since 1997, Weah has invested much time and money helping to build schools and clinics in his war-torn home country, Liberia.

FACTFILE In 1996, George Weah paid for his team-mates' kit and expenses so that Liberia could enter the African Nations Cup.

RONALDO
Brazil, born 1976
Caps: 98   Goals: 62

Ronaldo Luis Nazario de Lima became hot property as an 18-year-old by scoring 58 goals in just 60 games for Brazil's Cruzeiro. Ronaldo moved to PSV Eindhoven and then Barcelona, where his close control and devastating bursts of pace helped him become Europe's top scorer in 1996–97, with 34 goals. Sold to Internazionale, he was their top scorer in his first season. He then endured four injury-ravaged years. After a poor World Cup final in 1998, many doubted his ability, but he bounced back in 2002 as the tournament's top scorer. A month later, Real Madrid paid £28.49 million for the Brazilian, and in 2006 Ronaldo became the highest scorer in World Cup history, with 15 goals. In 2007, he moved to Italian giants AC Milan, and in 2009 to Brazilian team Corinthians.

FACTFILE
Ronaldo's ex-wife, Milene Domingues, broke the world record for keeping a football off the ground in 1995. She kept the ball in the air for nine hours and six minutes, making 55,187 touches in the process.

▼ *Ronaldo shows his pace against Italy. In 2002, he won his third FIFA World Player of the Year award.*

MIA HAMM
USA,
born 1972
Caps: 276
Goals: 158

Born with a partial club foot that had to be corrected by plaster casts, Mia Hamm went on to become the world's most famous female footballer. She was the youngest ever player for the US women's team when she debuted against China at the age of 15, and the youngest member of the US side that won the 1991 World Cup. Hamm played in three more World Cups, as well as winning two Olympic gold medals and one silver. A phenomenal all round player with an icy-cool finish, she was the leading scorer in the history of women's international football for a decade. Hamm was also a founding member of WUSA, playing for Washington Freedom when the league began in 2001.

HENRIK LARSSON
Sweden, born 1971
Caps: 104   Goals: 37

A goalscoring predator, Larsson played in Sweden before being signed by Feyenoord manager Wim Jansen in 1993. Four years later Jansen, by then the manager of Celtic, signed him again. Larsson became the Scottish Premier League's most feared striker, with 28 or more goals in five of his seven seasons. He retired from internationals in 2002, but changed his mind to help Sweden qualify for Euro 2004. Larsson then moved to Barcelona. In his final match for the Spanish side, the 2006 Champions League final, he came on as a substitute to play a key role in Barcelona's win. The striker returned to his former side, Helsingborg, before moving to Manchester United on loan in 2007.

◀ *The legendary Mia Hamm playing for the USA at the Women's Gold Cup in 2002. In the final against Canada, her golden goal in extra time secured the trophy.*

MARTA VIEIRA DA SILVA
Brazil, born 1986
Caps: 101   Goals: 105

Short for a striker, at under 1.6m tall, Marta is a goal-scoring dynamo who was voted the world's best female player five years in a row (2006–10). She played her early football for several Brazilian clubs before two spells in Sweden, either side of three seasons in the USA, where she won the Women's Professional Soccer (WPS) championship twice with two different clubs – FC Gold Pride and Western New York Flash. A truly prolific finisher, who averages more than a goal per game in club football, Marta has also won four Swedish league titles with Umeå IK, one with Tyresö FF and the 2014 title with FC Rosengård.

◀ *Barcelona's Henrik Larsson battles for the ball in a friendly against Japan's Kashima Antlers.*

PELÉ
Brazil, born 1940
Caps: 92 Goals: 77

Edson Arantes do Nascimento simply had it all. Considered the finest footballer of all time, Pelé was a masterful attacker with seemingly limitless skills, creativity and vision. He was magnificent in the air, lethal on the ground, could dribble, pass and take swerving free kicks, and saw passes and opportunities that other players could not. His father had been a striker for Fluminense, and at 11 years of age Pelé was spotted by a former Brazil player, Waldemar de Brito, who took him to Clube Atletico Bauru. Four years later, Pelé trialled at Santos, for whom he made his debut aged 15. He would play for the São Paulo side for the next 18 years. Pelé was only 17 when he appeared at the 1958 World Cup, scoring a hat-trick in the semi-final and two superb goals in the final as Brazil won their first World Cup. A pulled muscle cut short Pelé's involvement in the 1962 competition and he had to be content with winning the World Club Cup for Santos. Injured by brutal tackling in the 1966 World Cup, Pelé was outstanding at the 1970 tournament. He retired from international football in 1971 – in front of around 180,000 fans at the Maracana Stadium – and from

club football in 1974. In tribute, Santos removed the number ten shirt from their team line-up.

Pelé later came out of retirement to play in a star-studded line-up at New York Cosmos. He went on to become Brazil's minister of sport and a UN and UNICEF ambassador. He remains one of the most respected figures in world football and, in 1999, he was voted Athlete of the Century by the International Olympic Committee.

▶ *Pelé battles for the ball with an Italian defender at the 1970 World Cup.*

> **FACTFILE** Pelé's father once scored five headed goals in one game, a feat Pelé never managed. However, his header in the 1970 World Cup final was Brazil's 100th World Cup goal.

MATCH ACTION

Against Uruguay in the 1970 World Cup semi-final, Pelé came close to scoring what would have been one of the greatest goals ever seen. A through pass from Gerson saw Pelé and the Uruguayan keeper, Ladislao Mazurkiewicz, racing for the ball just outside the penalty area. Pelé made an outrageous dummy to the left, letting the ball run to the other side of the bewildered keeper. The striker sprinted to collect the ball and hit a first-time shot from a tight angle. The ball sped past Uruguayan defender Atilio Ancheta, only to flash mere centimetres wide of the left post.

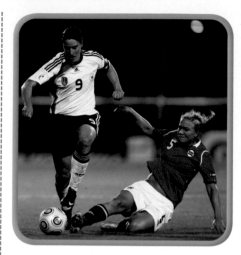

▲ *Germany's Birgit Prinz is challenged by Norway's Anneli Giske during the UEFA Women's Euro 2009.*

BIRGIT PRINZ
Germany, born 1977
Caps: 214 Goals: 128

Apart from a spell in the United States in 2002, where her 12 goals in 15 games helped Carolina Courage to win the WUSA championship, Prinz played all her club football for FFC Frankfurt. Here, she won six German league titles, eight German cups and scored over 250 goals (at a rate better than a goal a game). With Germany, she won two World Cups (2003, 2007), five European Championships and three Olympic bronze medals – a staggering haul. She was also awarded the FIFA World Women's Footballer of the Year on three occasions and finished second a further four times, the last in 2010, a year before she announced her retirement.

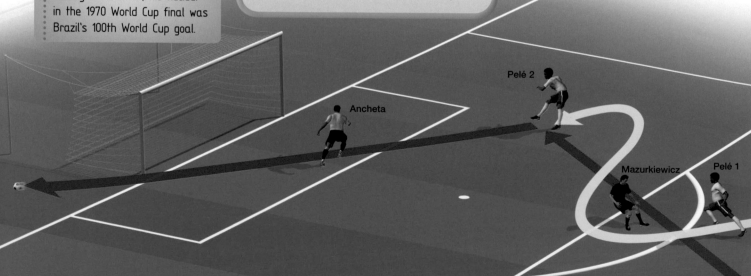

Pelé 2

Ancheta

Mazurkiewicz   Pelé 1

GABRIEL BATISTUTA
Argentina, born 1969
Caps: 77 Goals: 56

Batistuta played one season for each of his home country's three biggest clubs – Newell's Old Boys, River Plate and Boca Juniors – before moving to Italy in 1991, the year of his international debut. In nine seasons and 269 games at Fiorentina, the striker was rarely off-form, netting 168 goals. He even stayed with the club after relegation, helping them win promotion back into Serie A. In 2000, he joined Roma for the huge fee of £22 million. There Batistuta finally won the Serie A title in 2001. A winner of two Copa Americas, Batistuta scored five goals at the 1998 World Cup as Argentina made the quarter-finals. The 2003–04 season saw him make a lucrative move to Qatar, where he played for Al Arabi.

▲ *Argentina's all-time top scorer, Batistuta began the 1994–95 season by netting in each of Fiorentina's first 11 games, a Serie A record.*

LEADING INTERNATIONAL GOALSCORERS (TO MAY 2017)

PLAYER	COUNTRY	CAPS	GOALS
Ali Daei	Iran	149	109
Ferenc Puskas	Hungary	84	83
Godfrey Chitalu	Zambia	111	79
Hussein Mohammed	Iraq	137	78
Pelé	Brazil	92	77
Bashar Abdullah	Kuwait	134	75
Sandor Kocsis	Hungary	68	75
Majed Abdullah	Saudi Arabia	139	71
Miroslav Klose	Germany	113	71
Kiatisuk Senamuang	Thailand	134	71
Kinna Phiri	Malawi	115	71
Stern John	Trinidad & Tobago	115	70

MARCO VAN BASTEN
Holland, born 1964
Caps: 58 Goals: 24

One of the coolest finishers in world football, van Basten was just 29 when an ankle injury in the 1993 European Cup final effectively ended his playing career – although he struggled on until 1995. Renowned for spectacular goals in crucial contests, van Basten was European Footballer of the Year three times (1988, 1989 and 1992) and in 1988 he hit the headlines as Holland won the European Championships. He scored a hat-trick against England in the quarter-final, the semi-final winner versus Germany and a breathtaking volley from the tightest of angles in the final against the Soviet Union. With Ajax he won three league titles, scoring 128 goals. He then moved to AC Milan, hitting 90 goals in 147 games and winning three Serie A titles and two European Cups.

▶ *Marco van Basten on the rampage in Holland's 3-1 win over England at Euro '88.*

HUGO SANCHEZ
Mexico, born 1958
Caps: 57 Goals: 26

Mexico's most famous player, Sanchez spent the peak of his playing career in Spain, scoring over 230 goals for Atlético Madrid and Real Madrid. He formed a lethal partnership with Emilio Butragueno at Real as they won five league titles in a row. Sanchez was La Liga's top scorer in five different seasons and in 1990 he won the European Golden Boot for a record 38 goals in one season. Sadly, his commitments to European football and frequent bust-ups with Mexican football officials meant that he appeared in only a fraction of the international games played by his home country. He had a disappointing tournament at the 1986 World Cup on home soil, scoring just one goal.

> **FACTFILE** Playing for Manchester City in 1974, Denis Law scored a cheeky backheeled goal but did not celebrate – because the goal relegated his former club, Manchester United.

▲ *Denis Law unleashes a shot during a 1974 World Cup game against Zaire.*

DENIS LAW
Scotland, born 1940
Caps: 55 Goals: 30

In 1962, Manchester United paid £115,000 – a world record at the time – to bring the former Huddersfield Town, Manchester City and Torino striker Denis Law to Old Trafford. The money was well spent, as the quick-witted Scot formed a magnificent forward line with Bobby Charlton and George Best, scoring 160 goals in 222 games for the club. Fast over the ground and brave in the air, Law won the 1964 European Footballer of the Year award, as well as league titles and the European Cup with Manchester United, before moving to Manchester City and then retiring in 1974.

MARADONA'S WORLD CUP

Diego Maradona, the Argentinian striker with magical balance and touch, ended the 1986 World Cup with his hands on the trophy and a highly impressive five goals and five assists. Yet these statistics do not tell the story of his true impact, for Mexico '86 was Maradona's tournament. He roused a relatively ordinary Argentinian side into recapturing football's biggest prize (the South Americans had won the trophy on home soil in 1978) and wiped out the memory of a disappointing tournament in 1982.

In a tense quarter-final against England, controversy raged over Maradona's infamous 'Hand of God' goal (see right), but his second and winning goal was pure genius. The Argentinian collected the ball in his own half, then dribbled, twisted and turned through the English defence to score what was later voted the goal of the century. He would score a goal of similar brilliance in the semi-final versus Belgium. At this point, at the age of just 25, Maradona was without doubt the greatest footballer on the planet.

Diego Maradona, clutching the World Cup after his team's epic 3-2 victory over West Germany in the 1986 final, is carried around the Azteca Stadium on the shoulders of ecstatic Argentinian supporters.

► Maradona uses his hand to get the ball past England goalkeeper Peter Shilton to score Argentina's first goal in a 2-1 victory.

THE BRAIN GAME

Football is a sport that calls for pace, power, stamina and skill, but it also demands mental agility. Footballers with the ability to think one step ahead of the opposition are highly prized, and such skills can win a match for their team. The same applies to managers and coaches. In the run-up to a match, they have several key decisions to make. They must decide who to select, which formation to play, and choose the tactics they will use in their bid to outwit the opposition.

TEAM SELECTION

To a casual spectator, team selection appears simple – just pick the team's best 11 footballers and tell them to play. With large squads of players, the truth is far more complex. Teams need flair, skill, composure, aggression, sound defensive skills and goalscoring abilities – all in the right quantities. Some players, despite being footballing superstars, may not play well with each other or work with the rest of the team, while other, less heralded players may actually perform a more effective job in a particular game. The way the opposition plays can dictate which players are selected, as can the fitness and performances of individuals. Star players, who would normally be first on the team sheet, may not be picked if they are recovering from injury or suffering from a lack of confidence or form. Both young, talented players emerging from the reserve team and experienced veterans at the end of their careers will have strong cases for a place in the side. It all adds up

▲ *In the past, club squads were much smaller. In 1983–84, Liverpool's league- and European Cup-winning team (above) played 66 games with a squad of just 16. Bruce Grobbelaar, Alan Kennedy, Sammy Lee and Alan Hansen played in every game.*

▼ *West Germany manager Josef 'Sepp' Herberger (right) is chaired off the field as his team wins the 1954 World Cup. Early in the competition, he sent out a weakened side that lost to favourites Hungary. Having already beaten Turkey, Herberger's gamble meant that his side got an easier draw, meeting Turkey again in a play-off that the Germans won 7-2.*

to a complex puzzle that managers must solve. As the legendary Ajax and Holland coach Rinus Michels said, 'It is an art in itself to compose a starting team, finding the balance between creative players and those with destructive powers, and between defence, construction and attack – never forgetting the quality of the opposition and the specific pressures of each match.'

PICKING AND PLAYING

Picking the right players for the game ahead can be a tricky task. Managers are often criticized by fans for dropping a favourite player or not playing them in their favoured position. But they have to hold their nerve and go with what they feel is their best team for a particular match. Cesar Luis Menotti was criticized by the Argentinian public and media for refusing to include the teenage prodigy Maradona in his 1978 World Cup squad, fielding veteran striker Mario Kempes instead. But Menotti proved himself to be a strong-willed and clever coach, who surprised opponents with an exciting, attacking approach, and his team went on to beat Holland in the final.

With large squads, coaches at the top sides often rotate and rest key players. In games against supposedly weaker opposition, they might field an understrength side. While resting your best players and giving youngsters first-team experience can bring benefits, it is a risky tactic. Liverpool manager, Jurgen Klopp, rested key players and made nine changes for his side's 2017 FA Cup match vs Wolverhampton Wanderers, who play a division lower. Liverpool were knocked out of the competition, 2-1.

> **FACTFILE** FIFA changed its rules on substitutions in international friendlies in 2004, limiting a side to six subs. The move was prompted, in part, by the mass substitutions of England coach Sven-Goran Eriksson. In 2003, he made 11 substitutions during a game that Australia won 3-1.

SUBSTITUTIONS

Although they were allowed in some friendly matches, substitutes were not a feature of competitive games until the 1960s. Before this time, the lack of subs resulted in all sorts of heroics, from outfield players going in goal to footballers playing on in spite of a serious injury. One of the most famous examples is that of Manchester City's German goalkeeper

Bert Trautmann, who continued playing in the 1956 FA Cup final even though he had broken his neck. Today's managers have the chance to alter their team selection and tactics by making up to three substitutions in most competitions (more in friendly games). The timing and choice of substitutes can be crucial. They can bolster a winning side's momentum, help a defence to hold on to a lead or turn a losing team's fortunes around. In the 2006 World Cup, for example, Australia were losing 1-0 to Japan. Coach Guus Hiddink brought on two substitutes, Tim Cahill and John Aloisi, who scored three goals between them in the last six minutes of the game to secure a 3-1 victory.

◀ Substitutes can make an immediate impact in some games. Kamil Kopunek celebrates after coming on as substitute and scoring with his very first touch for Slovakia, in their shock win over Italy at the 2010 World Cup.

▼ With Manchester United losing 1-0 to Bayern Munich in the 1999 Champions League final, Alex Ferguson brought on Norwegian striker Ole Gunnar Solskjaer in the 81st minute. After another substitute, Teddy Sheringham, had equalized, Solskjaer scored this memorable winner in injury time.

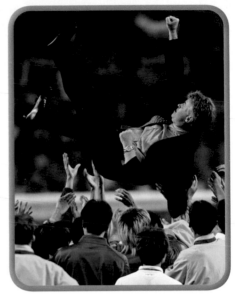

▲ After leading South Korea to the semi-finals of the 2002 World Cup, Dutchman Guus Hiddink – a firm believer in attacking tactics – was made an honorary citizen of South Korea.

FORMATIONS

The way in which a team lines up on the pitch is known as its formation. The first football international, in 1872, saw two sides field heavily attacking formations. Scotland began playing in a 2-2-6 formation, with two backs, two half-backs (similar to midfielders) and six attackers. England went even further, playing 1-1-8 (eight forwards), but crowded goalmouths saw the game end 0-0.

EVOLVING TACTICS

Although England's eight forwards quickly became a thing of the past, attacker-heavy formations such as 2-3-5 persisted for over half a century. A change to the offside law in 1925 (see page 19) reduced the number of players needed between an attacker and the goal from three to two. It gave attackers more scoring chances and forced a rapid rethink for managers. None was quicker than Arsenal's Herbert Chapman, who, two days after a 7-0 loss to Newcastle, debuted his W-M formation (so named for the shapes the two groups of five players made). The change resulted in a 4-0 win over West Ham. The W-M formation was effectively 3-2-2-3 and was adopted by many sides. Other teams played the *metodo* formation, devised by World Cup-winning Italian coach Vittorio Pozzo. It was also based on 2-3-5, but was effectively 2-3-2-3, with two of the forwards pulled back to link between midfield and attack and to defend against breaks by the opposition.

FOUR AT THE BACK

The arrival of four defenders at the back sounds like a negative formation, but it was first unveiled by the marvellous attacking Brazil side that won the 1958 World Cup. The Brazilian formation was actually 4-2-4, with two wingers up front feeding two central strikers. By the next World Cup, Brazil and many other sides were opting for a slightly less attacking 4-3-3 with an extra player to stop the midfield from being overrun. This formation can work with a single winger who switches flanks at will or with two genuine wingers feeding a single striker. England won the 1966 World Cup playing 4-4-2 with no out-and-out wingers, but they had midfielders with the energy and stamina to add width to an attack, as well as tucking in

◄ Playing as a wing-back, Germany's Philipp Lahm holds off Portugal's Cristiano Ronaldo. Wing-backs play on the flanks. They act like full-backs in defence, but also make attacking runs upfield.

to defend when necessary. This formation is still widely used today. Ahead of the four-man defence, a coach has plenty of options. He may opt for three attackers upfront (4-3-3) or split strikers (4-4-1-1) or no strikers at all. At the final of Euro 2012, Spain did away with out-and-out strikers, starting the game with three attacking midfielders – David Silva, Cesc Fabregas and Andrés Iniesta – instead of a regular centre-forward. They beat Italy convincingly, 4-0.

◄ Josep Guardiola directs one of his Barcelona players from the touchline. In 2013, he became head coach at Bayern Munich.

▲ The Serbia and Montenegro international Sinisa Mihajlovic enjoyed six glorious seasons at Lazio as a powerful sweeper, strong in defence but with an eye for goal, especially from set pieces.

SWEEPING UP

At many clubs around the world, and in Italian football especially, a different system is used at the back, with a sweeper (also known as a *libero* or 'free man') in the centre of defence. Sweepers tend to play behind the main line of defenders, literally sweeping up loose balls and acting as a last line of defence if an opposition attack breaks through. In some formations, a sweeper can be ultra-negative. This was seen as the case with the *catenaccio* system, invented by Padova coach Nereo Rocco in the early 1950s and popularized by Helenio Herrera's Internazionale side of the 1960s. Effectively

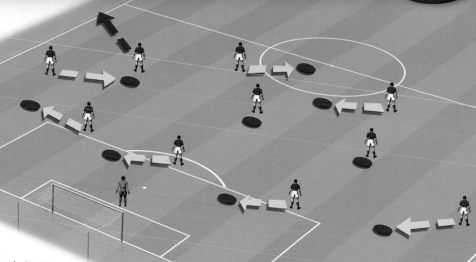

▲ Celebrated coach José Mourinho has won league titles in four countries: Portugal, Italy, England and Spain. After winning the league three times with Chelsea, Mourinho became manager for Manchester United in 2016.

a 1-4-3-2 or 1-4-4-1 system, *catenaccio* aimed to stifle attacks with large numbers of defenders, relying on counterattacks by a few forwards. Italy has produced a long line of world-class sweepers including Giovanni Facchetti, Gaetano Scirea and Franco Baresi. But it took a German, Franz Beckenbauer, to show a different side to

▲ A team often alters its formation after a sending-off. This side has lost its left midfielder (shown by the red arrow) and switches from a 3-2-3-2 system with wing-backs to a 4-3-1-1 formation with a flat back four, three in midfield and split strikers up front.

the sweeper's art. Beckenbauer linked play going forward and would often surge ahead of his defence, creating an extra player in

FACTFILE Ronald Koeman is one of the highest-scoring defenders of all time. Playing mostly as a sweeper, he enjoyed great success with AC Milan, Barcelona and Holland, scoring an incredible 193 goals in 533 games.

attack and opening up the game.

Today, the sweeper is often replaced by one or more deep-sitting midfielders, one of whom can drop back into defence if a defender pushes forwards. These 'anchor' or defensive midfielders – such as Spain's Sergio Busquets or France's N'Golo Kanté – are highly prized.

TOTAL FOOTBALL

'Total football' was never quite formation-free football, but it did involve players switching positions and roles within the team with amazing frequency. Under Rinus Michels, defenders would crop up in attack, strikers in midfield and midfielders just about everywhere. It proved a hard system to defend against, but few sides could boast the quality of player to make it work, as it relied on excellent ball skills and very high energy levels. Today, players switch positions with remarkable ease and regularity, so much so that one might wonder why total football caused such a stir. Formations in the past were more rigid, however, with full-backs staying in their half and strikers staying upfield throughout the game. While this gave a team a shape and structure, it could also make it easier for opponents to mark dangerous players and defend.

FORMATIONS

A formation is the way in which a team lines up for a match. This is usually shown in terms of the numbers of outfield players from the defence forwards. In reality, football is a dynamic game and players move around the pitch. Sometimes, they are drawn out of position by an opposition attack. At other times, players choose to move out of position. For example, a central striker may drift out wide or drop back to find space.

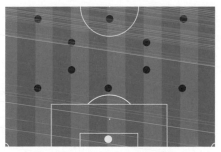

3-2-2-3 formation

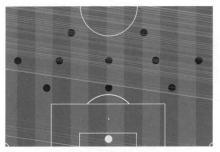

3-5-2 formation

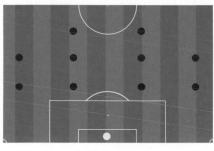

4-4-2 formation

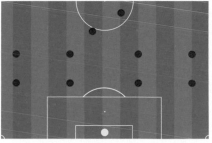

4-4-1-1 formation

TACTICS

Teams may kick off a game in one of several common formations, but there can be great variation in how they play within that formation and in the tactics they use. For example, a team that lines up as a 4-4-2 side may choose to play defensively, with midfielders tucking in, or aggressively, with one or more midfielders joining the strikers in attack.

TAILORING TACTICS

Managers start a game with what they feel are the best tactics for the players available and the opposition they face. They watch how a match unfolds closely, knowing they can change tactics at any time to exploit an opponent's weakness or to fix problems in their own team's play. Most top footballers can play in several positions. A manager may switch formations using the same players or bring on a substitute with different attributes and skills. In the 2014 World Cup, Netherlands coach Louis van Gaal brought on substitute goalkeeper Tim Krul purely for the penalty shootout with Costa Rica. Krul saved two penalties as the Netherlands won. A year later, at the 2015 Women's World Cup semi-final versus Germany, US coach Jill Ellis changed her usual 4-4-2 formation, switching to a 4-2-3-1, which helped her side triumph 2-0.

TACTICS IN DEFENCE

Teams have several choices about how they defend. Some managers prefer defenders to patrol areas of space that overlap, a system known as zonal marking. This tactic is often used by Argentinian clubs and many national sides. It requires good communication between defenders. Alternatively, each defender marks an individual player, tracking their opponent's attacking runs throughout the game. Manchester United's Phil Jones, for example, man-marked Real Madrid's Cristiano Ronaldo during their 2013 Champions League game, restricting his chances on the ball in a 1-1 draw. When an opposing team features a dangerous playmaker positioned behind the strikers, a side may nominate an extra central defender to man-mark him or her.

▲ Clint Dempsey heads the ball during the 2011 CONCACAF Gold Cup final between the USA and Mexico. Versatile players such as Dempsey, who can play up front or in several positions in midfield, give a coach more options to change formations and tactics during a game.

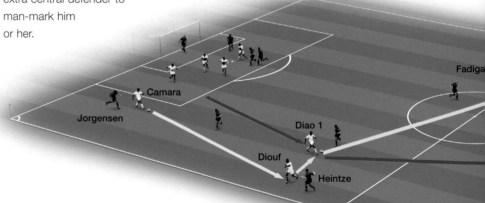

▶ The offside trap is a defensive tactic in which the back three or four players move upfield in a straight line to catch an opponent offside. It can be very effective, but may be beaten by a player dribbling through the line or by a well-timed through pass combined with an attacking run.

MATCH ACTION

A goal down and under pressure from a Danish attack down their right wing, Senegal scored a superb counter-attacking goal at the 2002 World Cup. Senegal's Henri Camara made a firm tackle on Martin Jorgensen and played a quick pass down the wing to El Hadji Diouf. Diouf, closely marked by Jan Heintze, spotted Salif Diao's run and backheeled the ball into his path. Diao hit a perfect pass to Khalilou Fadiga, who was sprinting into the centre circle. As Diao continued his run, Fadiga took the ball into the Danish half before playing a perfectly timed through pass. Racing between two defenders, Diao latched onto the ball and coolly dispatched it into the corner of the goal.

LONG OR SHORT

All teams seek to pass and move the ball into the attacking third of the pitch, where goalscoring chances can be fashioned. The way in which they get the ball there can vary greatly. For many decades, British managers believed that hitting long balls towards tall target strikers in the opponent's penalty area created more goal chances, often through a defensive mistake. In continental Europe and elsewhere, a shorter passing-and-moving game was often preferred, with sides keeping possession for relatively long periods as they looked for an opening in the opposition defence. Another tactic is to rely on pinpoint passing and skilful dribbling to get into the opposition penalty area. Some teams play a counter-attacking game, defending in large numbers and soaking up pressure. When they retrieve the ball, they move it rapidly out of defence with a long pass or by running with the ball. Fast, accurate counter-attacking can catch the opposition off guard and outnumbered, but requires players with good pace and awareness. Many coaches mix up their passing and movement tactics – if their team is behind with only minutes to go, they may switch to a direct style, pushing extra players up into the opposition penalty area to look for headers and knock-downs.

◄ Cristiano Ronaldo practises free kicks at a Portuguese training camp. Attacking set pieces are often planned and worked on hard in training as they offer a good chance of scoring.

HIT THE NET

http://performance.fourfourtwo.com/tactics
A collection of great tactical tips and videos from leading coaches.

www.thefalse9.com/category/football-tactics-for-beginners
A great series of articles on different aspects of tactics, from keeping compact in defence to how to counter-attack and the role of full-backs.

www.football-lineups.com/tactic/4-3-1-2
Diagrams and comments on more than 20 different formations used by teams.

FACTFILE
Barcelona lost the first leg of their 2017 UEFA Champions League quarter-final versus Paris Saint-Germain 4–0. In an astonishing comeback, they won the second leg, 6–1, to go through.

► Russia's Andrei Arshavin (left) often plays as a second striker behind a front centre-forward. His opponent, Xavi Hernandez, is a midfielder who sometimes moves forward to join attacks.

Fadiga 2

Diao 2

THE MANAGER'S ROLE

A successful team needs more than great tactics. It needs to be prepared, instructed and inspired to produce a great performance. Motivating players, directing them and giving them the confidence to perform is all part of a manager's job. Crucially, managers can determine the tone, style and attitude of their side through the players they buy and send out onto the pitch, as well as through their work on the training ground.

THE TEAM BEHIND THE TEAM

Behind the footballers at a major club or national side is a large team of staff. At the helm is the manager and his assistant coaches, some of whom may specialize in training goalkeepers or strikers, or may specifically work with younger players and youth teams. A top club will also include a fitness coach, a dietician and one or more physiotherapists and medical staff to help with players' preparation and injury

▲ *José Mourinho oversees a training session before Real Madrid's 2013 Champions League quarter-final against Galatasaray. Head coaches like Mourinho are in charge of an array of coaches and physios, as well as fitness and diet experts.*

recovery. Videos of games that interest the management are studied in detail, while scouts are employed to check out and report on forthcoming opposition sides and to watch potential transfer targets in action. Many clubs and national teams also arrange visits from temporary personnel such as sports psychologists, balance and co-ordination specialists, as well as inspirational figures from other sports.

INS AND OUTS

With football clubs becoming increasingly big businesses, a manager's ability to deal profitably and successfully in the transfer market is essential. Some managers are highly prized for their ability to buy players cheaply and sell them for profit or to put together a team on a limited budget that can seriously challenge for honours. European Cup-winning manager Brian Clough was famous for working wonders with bargain buys such as Scottish legend Archie Gemmill, who cost Clough's Derby side £66,000. Many clubs today still have an eye for a bargain. Leicester City, for example, bought Riyad Mahrez for £400,000 and N'Golo Kanté for £5.6 million and sold the latter in 2016 to Chelsea for £32 million. Tottenham Hotspur made an even larger profit after buying Gareth Bale from Southampton for a total fee of £7 million in 2007 and selling him in 2013 to Real Madrid for £83.3 million. Other managers are rated for their ability

▶ *In 2011, Porto bought Radamel Falcao from Argentinean club River Plate for less than £4 million. After three seasons, in which he scored 72 goals in 87 games, they sold him on to Atletico Madrid for approximately ten times what they had originally paid.*

FACTFILE Irishman Tony Cascarino was sold in 1982 by Crockenhill FC to Gillingham for a new club strip and some corrugated iron to patch up the ground. The total cost was said to be £180.

to bring promising youngsters through from their youth set-ups or training academies, and to attract good players on loan from other clubs to help strengthen their side at key stages of the season.

UNDER PRESSURE

Few people in sport are under as much pressure as the manager of a major club or national side. Managers stand or fall by their results. In the past, some managers stayed at clubs for season after season. Miguel Munoz, for example, managed Real Madrid for 417 games during the 1960s. At the top level today, few coaches stay in charge of the best teams for more than a handful of seasons. In the 2015–16 season, 66 of the 92 professional English league clubs changed managers. In 2007, Leroy Rosenior became manager of Torquay United but

new owners arrived at the same time. As a result, he was sacked after just ten minutes in charge. Even recent success does not guarantee a long stay. Real Madrid's Vicente del Bosque had delivered two Spanish league titles, two Champions League trophies and other cups to the Spanish giants in just four years, but was dismissed in June 2003. In 2008, Roberto Mancini was sacked as head coach of Internazionale straight after delivering the club its third Serie A title in a row. In such an unforgiving climate, Alex Ferguson's record of over 1,500 games in charge of Manchester United is quite remarkable.

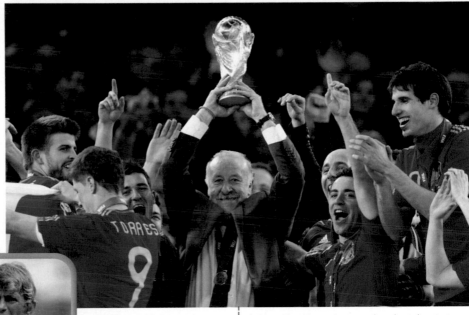

▲ *Vicente del Bosque holds the World Cup after guiding Spain to victory in 2010. A former Real Madrid player and manager, he was voted World Coach of the Year in 2012.*

◀ *Bora Milutinovic led five different countries to successive World Cups – a unique feat in football management. In 2009, he was appointed coach of Iraq.*

FACTFILE
In a 1999 Spanish second division game, Leganes manager Enrique Martin run onto the pitch to haul down an opposition player who was clean through on goal. Martin received a ten-match ban.

MANAGERIAL MIGRATIONS

Like modern players, top managers often move abroad to further their coaching careers. Whilst teams such as Germany and Italy have never had a foreign coach, more and more have, including England with Sven-Goran Eriksson and Fabio Capello. In the past, British coaches were influential abroad. Willy Garbutt helped shape Genoa into a powerful side, while Fred Pentland coached Athletic Bilbao to Spanish league success in 1930 and 1931. Jimmy Hogan, who used pass-and-move tactics years ahead of his time, worked with Austrian coaching legend Hugo Miesl to set up the Vienna School of attractive football. This created the Austrian *Wunderteam* that remained unbeaten in 14

internationals and narrowly missed out on glory at the 1934 World Cup and 1936 Olympics. Today, managers and coaches swap countries and continents frequently. Dutch coach Guus Hiddink managed many European clubs as well as the national teams of the Netherlands, South Korea, Australia, Russia and Turkey, whilst Italian manager Fabio Capello has coached England and, from 2012, the Russian national team. Globetrotting Luis Felipe Scolari has managed 21 clubs all over the world from China and Qatar to England and Uzbekistan. He has also coached Portugal, Kuwait and Brazil twice.

▼ *Jürgen Klinsmann was appointed head coach of the US men's team in 2011 and led them to nine wins in 2012, including a victory over Italy. The former German striker had only one season as a club manager (Bayern Munich, 2008–09).*

▲ *Globetrotting Frenchman Philippe Troussier has successfully coached and managed Nigeria, South Africa, Japan, China and clubs in Europe.*

GREAT MANAGERS

There have been dozens of truly great managers and coaches in football. Some have been masters at discovering new talents and putting together successful teams on tight budgets; others are football visionaries who have helped to improve the skills and play of the world's biggest stars. Below are profiles of eight of the finest managers in the history of football.

HERBERT CHAPMAN
1878-1934

Only four teams have won the English league three seasons in a row, and Chapman created two of them. After arriving at Huddersfield Town in 1921, he won the league in 1924 and 1925. By the time Huddersfield made it three in a row, Chapman had left for Arsenal. They were in 20th place when he took over, but finished the season second, behind his former side. Arsenal went on to win a hat-trick of league titles, the first two under Chapman. The Englishman took tactics very seriously, and his W-M formation (see page 60) was taken up by many sides. He pioneered large-scale youth coaching, undersoil heating, top-class medical facilities and professional training regimes. Some of his proposals, such as numbered shirts and playing regular evening games under floodlights, were adopted only long after his death.

GIOVANNI TRAPATTONI
Born 1939

Trapattoni's managerial career got off to a flying start, winning the 1973 European Cup-Winners' Cup as caretaker manager of AC Milan, for whom he had played as a fearsome centre-back. After moving to Milan's great rivals Juventus, he enjoyed an unmatched run of success, winning six Serie A league titles, two UEFA Cups and, in 1985, a European Cup. Trapattoni won a further Serie A title with Internazionale in 1989 before moving to Bayern Munich in the 1990s, where he became the first foreign manager to win the Bundesliga. His teams were based on strong defences, usually with three central defenders and exciting attackers who were often bought from abroad. He was finally given a chance to coach the Italian national side at 63 years of age, but the team fell short at the 2002 World Cup and Euro 2004, after which Trapattoni had spells at Benfica, Stuttgart and Salzburg. Between 2008 and 2013, he was coach of the Republic of Ireland national team.

▲ *Trapattoni argues with the officials during Italy's match against Bulgaria at Euro 2004.*

BELA GUTTMANN
1900-81

The only manager to have won the top club trophy in both South America and Europe, Guttmann is a coaching legend. He was a gifted amateur player for MTK Budapest and appeared at the 1924 Olympics for Hungary. After retiring in 1935, he embarked on a 40-year-long coaching career that took him to Switzerland, Uruguay, Greece, Portugal, Brazil, Romania, Italy and Austria. He won national league titles in five different countries, including the 1955 Serie A title with AC Milan; he won the European Cup twice as coach of Benfica and also lifted the Copa Libertadores with Peñarol. He was a great influence on Gusztav Sebes, the coach of the magical Hungarian sides of the 1950s, and his forward-thinking 4-2-4 formation and styles of play are believed to have inspired Brazil to become the great attacking force of the late 1950s onwards.

JOCK STEIN
1922-85

Jock Stein began his coaching career as assistant manager at Celtic. In 1960, he moved to Dunfermline and beat his old club in the following season to win the Scottish Cup. In 1962, Dunfermline caused a major upset, knocking out top Spanish side Valencia from the Inter-Cities Fairs Cup. Stein moved on to Hibernian for a season before being appointed as the boss of Celtic. He quickly built one of British soccer's finest and most entertaining sides. Under Stein, Celtic won 11 Scottish league titles and, in 1967, overturned the mighty Internazionale to become the first British team to lift the European Cup. The 'Big Man' left Celtic in 1977 for an ill-fated spell at Leeds United, but later became Scotland's coach, guiding them to the 1982 and 1986 World Cup tournaments.

> **FACTFILE** In the 1970s, two managerial legends, Jock Stein and Brian Clough, both had spells at Leeds United that lasted just 44 days.

◀ *Herbert Chapman (right) watches an Arsenal match in 1932 alongside trainer Tom Whittaker (left) and star player Alex James.*

SIR ALEX FERGUSON
Born 1941

As European football's longest-serving top-flight manager, Sir Alex Ferguson has taken Manchester United to a record 13 Premier League titles and the 1999 and 2008 Champions League crowns. A ruthless and highly driven player, Ferguson carried those attributes into his managerial career, first with East Stirling and then at St Mirren and Aberdeen. He broke the monopoly of Celtic and Rangers to win three Scottish league titles; in 1983, his team defeated Real Madrid to lift the European Cup-Winners' Cup. Ferguson also served as assistant Scotland manager under Jock Stein, taking over in 1985. At Manchester United, Ferguson developed young talents such as David Beckham and Ryan Giggs, and proved to be a masterful player of mind games with rival managers. Knighted in 1999, for his services to the game, 'Sir' Alex announced his retirement from club management at the end of the 2012–13 season, after 26 years with Manchester United.

FACTFILE Alex Ferguson was sacked only once, in 1978, when Scottish club St Mirren fired him for a range of offences that included 'unpardonable swearing at a lady'.

RINUS MICHELS
1928–2005

The man behind 'total football', which revolutionized both Ajax and the Dutch national team, Marinus 'Rinus' Michels had been a centre-forward as a player, winning five caps for Holland in the 1950s. As coach of Ajax in the mid-1960s, he gave 17-year-old Johan Cruyff his debut. Michels later managed Cruyff at Spanish giants Barcelona and in the Dutch team that finished runners-up at the 1974 World Cup. Michels returned to Ajax in 1975 and became coach of German side Cologne five years later. He rejoined the Dutch national side in 1984 and, with a star-studded team, won the 1988 European Championships – Holland's first major trophy. Michels' achievements were acknowledged in 1989, when he was named FIFA's Coach of the Century.

VALERY LOBANOVSKY
1939–2002

A gifted mathematician, Valery Lobanovsky viewed football as a science, and was one of the first managers to analyse the performances of teams and players. His management style was strict, yet it enabled creative talents such as Oleg Blokhin and Andriy Shevchenko to flourish. After four years in charge of Dnipro Dnipropetrovsk, he was appointed coach of Dynamo Kiev, guiding them to five Soviet league titles between 1974 and 1981 and two European Cup-Winners' Cup victories (1975 and 1986). He also coached the Soviet Union in three spells, reaching the 1988 European Championships final, only to be defeated by Rinus Michels' Dutch team. After spells with the United Arab Emirates and Kuwait, he returned to Kiev in 1996, taking them to five Ukrainian league titles in a row (1997–2001) and reaching the semi-finals of the Champions League in 1999.

► Rinus Michels with Johan Cruyff during their time at Barcelona.

HELENIO HERRERA
1917–97

The well-travelled Argentinian Helenio Herrera was a tough manager who liked to control almost every aspect of a club. At Spain's Atlético Madrid, he won back-to-back league titles. After spells with Malaga, Valladolid and Sevilla, he joined Barcelona. Under his management, they won two Spanish titles and two Inter-Cities Fairs Cups. Internazionale liked what they saw and headhunted him in 1960. Herrera's reign and his use of *catenaccio* tactics (see page 60) coincided with Inter's most glorious era, in which they won three Serie A titles, two European Cups and two World Club Cups. Herrera was also in charge of the Italian national team during qualification for the 1962 World Cup, but by the time the tournament began, he was manager of Spain.

◄ In November 2004, Alex Ferguson celebrated his 1,000th game in charge of Manchester United by beating Lyon in the Champions League.

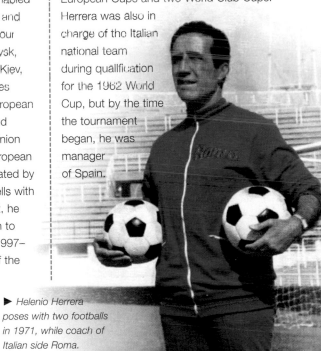
► Helenio Herrera poses with two footballs in 1971, while coach of Italian side Roma.

Lothar Emmerich of West Germany fires
a shot past England's George Cohen
(far left) and Martin Peters during the
epic 1966 World Cup final at Wembley.